# From Mazas to Jerusalem

**An Anarchist Outsider on the Run**

**Zo d'Axa**
**translated by Wolfi Landstreicher**

*From Mazas to Jerusalem: An Anarchist Outsider on the Run*

By Zo d'Axa

Translated by Wolfi Landstreicher

First Edition, Black Powder Press, 2017

ISBN 978-0-9994132-0-3

Cover design by Black Powder Press. Interior design by Margaret Killjoy.

# CONTENTS

**1**
**Introduction**

**3**
**Zo d'Axa's Heresy**

**15**
**One: Malefactor**

*Brigand Tale; Mazas; Interlude; In Solitary Confinement; "Comrade" Cop; Little Details Behind the Scenes; Provisional Liberty*

**39**
**Two: Incitement to Murder**

*Forward in Case of Absence*

## 47
## Three:
## English Holiday
*Tit for Tat; Socialist Babel; The Melville Gang;
Ta-ra-ra-boom-de-ay!*

## 63
## Four:
## The Long Trek
*No Matter Where; Traveling Musicians; The Barge; From
Cities to Country Villages; Young Girls; Know the Country!;
After Expulsion; The Useful Knife; Night Shelter; The Dogs of
Galatta; Spy; "Me consul"; He who trusts is crazy; The Escape;
Jerusalem; The Flag; For Murderers; At Sea; Black Sheep; The
Last Hotel*

## 133
## Five:
## From Both Sides
*False Exit; On the Street*

# Zo d'Axa

# de Mazas à Jérusalem

Zo d'Axa

# INTRODUCTION

*From Mazas to Jerusalem* is Zo d'Axa's account of his persecution by the authorities for daring to write and publish material favoring active and fierce rebellion against all authorities. More importantly it is an account of a rebellious individual who would not bow even in the face of such persecution.

Zo d'Axa, along with many other anarchists, was arrested and imprisoned in 1892 for writing and publishing articles considered a danger to the French Republic and for trying to raise funds to help the families of imprisoned anarchists. Shortly after his release, he again wrote something offensive to the French authorities and rather than face prison, he went on the lam. *From Mazas to Jerusalem* gives an often poetic, often amusing, often heart-rending account of his adventures during this time.

I have included my translation of the introduction to an Italian edition of this book that gives a strong feel for the depth of Zo d'Axa's rebellion which attacked not only the obvious authorities, but also the authority of radical and anarchist thought that had hardened into dogma and tradition based on a kind of quasi-religious apocalyptic faith in a coming "new dawn". For Zo d'Axa, rebellion was an *immediate* confrontation with the authorities that got in the way of his insistence on creating his life on his own terms without waiting for the coming of some revolutionary paradise. He was an outsider and a heretic even within anarchist circles … precisely because he was genuinely anarchic in his attitudes, ideas and practice. And by the end of the book, he decides to no longer call himself an anarchist, not because he has given up his rebellion, but because it is too large even for that word. He says instead calls himself "… a free man, a loner searching beyond; but not enthralled by a dream. Having the pride to affirm myself, outside of schools and sects … outside enslaving laws, outside narrow rules, even outside the theories ideally formulated for the coming age."

When looking at what is currently called "anarchist", I can relate to his refusal of this label. But for me it has always only been a name I use to express in one word my refusal to be ruled, to conform, to live me life on any terms other than my own. And Zo d'Axa lived that refusal deeply.

*Wolfi Landstreicher*

# ZO D'AXA'S HERESY

*Introductory essay to the Italian translation of* De Mazas à Jérusalem
*(From Mazas to Jerusalem)*

ACCORDING TO THE ETYMOLOGY OF THE WORD, A HERETIC IS one "who chooses", choice meant in the strongest of its accepted meanings, as active decision, certainly not in the bland dress of adjustment. A heretic is not one who limits himself to belonging, approving, following. Nor is he even one who is content to study, learn and repeat. A heretic is not one who knows the old answers by heart, but rather one who loves to formulate new questions. The heretic does not demand approval, but rather critique; he does not want to maintain, but to change. If the heretic usually doesn't go very far, a reproach that is often made against him, it is because he spends his time opening new paths rather than going down all too well-trodden ones.

There's no need to point out that heretics are not just found in religion. They are everywhere. So much so that one can confidently say that where the beacon of certainty shines in any field, there the shadow of doubt grows longer. Even social movements have often been shaken by the presence of heretics. A terror to the guardians of ideology, individuals of this kind are insulted, defamed and banished precisely like all other heretics. If they do not end up being burnt at the stake of the Inquisition, their names still get blacked out from most people's memories. And their merits have been hard to recognize, except in a few particular instances, many years after their deaths. As everyone knows, there is always time to raise a statue to Giordano Bruno in the public square.

Very few heard Zo d'Axa speak even among anarchists in whose movement he fought for years. He was barely known in France, his country of origin, and was nearly unheard of in the rest of the world. Aside from fragmentary bits of news (like his family ties to famous personalities) or the translation of some brilliant phrase (perhaps in favor of abstentionism) nearly nothing has reached us up to now. Zo d'Axa, you see, was a heretic, a heretic of the anarchist movement that has not always known how to practice that absolute freedom that it intended to realize, sometimes getting stuck in a thick web of dogmas, precepts and norms.

Zo d'Axa's name is linked to that of the weekly he founded and of which he was the managing editor. The journal was called *L'Endehors* (Outside). It's motto was: "The one who no one governs and who is guided exclusively by an impulsive nature, this passional whole, this outlaw, this alien to every school, this loner who seeks the elsewhere, isn't he indicated in the term: Outside?" It was published in Paris from May 1891 until February 1893 – years when the name of anarchy came to be associated with the thunder of dynamite. *L'Endehors* had some bizarre characteristics for a subversive periodical. It wasn't limited to publishing writings of known anarchists or those who were destined to become so – like Sébastien Faure, Louise Michel, Errico Malatesta, Charles Malato or Emile Henry. Alongside them, there were also writers, poets and journalists, some already known, others just starting—people like Georges Darien, Octave Mirbeau, Félix Fénéon, Saint-Paul-Roux and many more. All "deserters of the bourgeoisie" as d'Axa loved to call them.

The editors of *L'Endehors* were, in short, ravished by the temptation to open the communicating vessels between dream and action in a challenge that would provoke great upheavals in the years to come. Not by chance, in defiance of one of Baudelaire's bitter reflections, a great voice shouted from the pages of this weekly that "action is the sister of the dream". More an aspiration than an observation, it's no use to deny it, but no less meaningful for that. What's the use of acting if you don't have a dream to realize? To fall into the sorriest militancy? And what's the use of dreaming if you don't consequently act? To fall into the most innocuous aestheticism?

The attempt was perhaps the first of its kind to be carried forward in such an organic manner. Unfortunately, it did not give the results hoped for. Several factors contributed to its demise, not least of which was the heavy intervention of the police, who were quick to apply the "black laws" that the French government had passed, which closely resemble the current post-September 11, European [and America] anti-terrorism laws, in their fieriness in dispensing heavy-handed charges of "subversive association" to anyone who doesn't become an accomplice of the state. ("The government decided to take advantage of the emotions caused by the explosions... to include all active revolutionaries in a huge trial against intentions. The minister and his docile prosecutor have ended up holding that certain ideas constitute complicity. The writer who explains how so many of the disinherited are inevitably drawn to theft has himself become a thief simply for expressing these thoughts. The thinker who analyzes the reasons for 'propaganda by the deed' has become the secret accomplice of the one who lit the tragic fuse. The philosopher no longer has the right to declare his indulgence and consider the events without astonishment": is this the end of the 19th century or the beginning of the 21st?)

But perhaps Zo d'Axa's generous effort would have still been destined to drown in the stormy sea of misunderstanding. The greatest obstacle seems to have been precisely an anarchist movement firmly anchored to ideological orthodoxy, which saw such experiments in subversive alchemy as only a waste of time, if not a tool of reaction for diverting the interests of workers from the Just Cause. This refined judgment must have been widespread in the anarchist movement of the time, since it is found again a dozen years later repeated word-for-word in some well-known writings of Luigi Fabbri where the baleful "bourgeois influences on anarchism" are stigmatized as the work of drawing room literati, guilty of exalting acts of violence committed by anarchists. Even though Zo d'Axa's journal is never cited – Fabbri preferred to mention organs of anarchist literature such as, for example, *La Revue Blanche*, rather than those of "literary anarchy" as *L'Endehors* was considered – the reference to it was still obvious, since many of the collaborators in the journal end up under the critique of the Romagnolan anarchist. Of course, with the benefit of hindsight – Fabbri's texts were published in 1906-1907 – it was easy to lay into those literati who had offered their pen to anarchy in their youth only to pass over to the other side of the barricades (as if this had not also happened to many "rugged militants").

But what is most striking in Fabbri's interventions, aside from the hysterical tone with which he launches his cry of alarm, is the lack of a substantial foundation for his arguments as well as the inability to even sense the reasons for and potential development of such an experiment. Yes, because if, on the one hand, Fabbri doesn't seem to be aware that the literary panegyrics to the "*beau geste*" were a consequence of the anarchist attacks that happened in that historical period and certainly not one of their causes (a thing that shows at most that "anarchist influences on literature"), on the other hand, he shows that he knows how, is able and wants to accept only "the anarchy conceived by philosophers, economists and anarchist sociologists". But once reduced to mere speculations, calculations and observations – however much with the militant warranty label – what is left of the passionate content of anarchy, of a world finally free of power? Nothing; since everything else is swiftly liquidates as "bourgeois influence". Once this political anarchism, full of good sense, is only made clear, it is no surprise that Fabbri comes to condemn without appeal "this fever for new things, this spirit of audacity, this mania for the extraordinary that has drawn the most extremely impressionable types into the anarchist ranks" since "these elements contribute the most to discrediting the idea."

Well then, it is enough to compare such words with those of Bakunin ("There has always been a basic defect in my nature: love of the fantastic, of extraordinary and unheard-of adventure, of undertakings with boundless horizons the outcome of which no one can predict") in order to fully grasp the chasm that had been created in the anarchist movement toward the end of the 19th century, between those who wanted a freedom governed by reason (the sacred church) and those who wanted a freedom without reasons (the heresy). It is into this chasm that Zo d'Axa slid.

Indeed, *L'Endehors*, with its ostentatious exaltation of the individual in revolt, could only leave all those revolutionaries who were only capable of understand the mass march perplexed. Jean Maitron, well-known historian of the French anarchist movement, illustrated the embarassment that *L'Endehors* caused when he describes it as "so nihilistic that it even goes beyond anarchy, while defending its ideas and people." This also explains another description that accompanied Zo d'Axa to the end of his life, the one that wanted him to be an anarcho-aristocrat.

But of what did Zo d'Axa's nihilism and aristocratism consist? In a few words, his obstinate refusal to promise paradise to the exploited.

The problem is not as insignificant as it might seem. There has always been a great portion of the anarchist movement that strives to depict anarchy as a panacea for all the evils that afflict humanity, as a rich arcadia of love, happiness and equality. In the hope of being able to persuade the masses, all too often many anarchists have been compelled to represent the revolution as a redeeming light raised beyond the world in a blaze of blessedness. Zo d'Axa saw such promises as a sham and those who made them as crude hucksters. For him, it was not the desire to achieve a sublime ideal that was the point of departure for the will to affect the real and transform life, but rather the horror in what surrounded him. Any alternative project that aimed based on anti-authoritarian principles was therefore alien to him, because one cannot promise, much less support, what one does not know. It follows from this that his way of expressing himself did without the socio-economic analysis so dear to a certain type of revolutionary propaganda in need of objective confirmations, realistic proposals, efficient results.

Now, the absence of a prepackaged theory about descriptions of what the future might be certainly can't be defined as nihilism, since this term usually refers to a methodical devaluation of all values. And it is a crude error to think that giving up determining the future *a priori* means consigning it to the limbo of the void. In reality, Zo d'Axa did not believe that beyond this boorish life made of work, money and obedience there would be nothing: he simply did not know what might be there. A world without domination in all its manifestations is impossible to predict. Any attempt to plan it is nothing more than a rite for exorcizing the fear of the unknown.

When the young child finds himself in the dark, he sings in a high voice to give himself courage. In the same way, many aspiring subversives are accustomed to building hyperbolic theoretical social edifices in order to overcome the panic that grips them when they think about an existence without the securities that the most dreadful habit is still able to furnish to them. But up to what point are these projects of social reconstruction only the echo of the frightened child's lullaby? Worse still, to what extent are these plausible, cautious, rational projects merely the bait with which to attract the consent of the people?

It is against the lie of propaganda that Zo d'Axa's brutal sincerity lashes out: there isn't any future for which to survive and in which to hope, only a present in which to live and take pleasure. Like the Argonauts, Zo d'Axa knew that the most intense joy consists in living the adventures of the journey – whatever they are – not in the attainment of the Golden Fleece. This is why Zo d'Axa sang of the pleasure of revolt and mercilessly mocked the priests of the happy gospel.

Obviously, those who aim to convert the greatest number of people to the Ideal, it doesn't matter which one, bear this ironic attitude towards the truthfulness of their advertising slogans poorly. Especially when it comes from their own ranks. In order to defend themselves, many anarchists could find nothing better to do than to brand Zo d'Axa with nihilism, or with being a supporter of nothing. One promises paradise to the exploited as the just recompense for those who have suffered so much, so criticizing paradise is equated with criticizing the exploited as its addressees. And whoever criticizes the exploited – i.e., whoever permits himself to demolish their illusions, whoever dares to mock their gullibility – can only be an aristocrat, a nihilist, in the final analysis, an enemy. There is no need to dwell on the nonsense of such syllogisms.

Unlike other anarchists who found themselves, in a certain sense, in the same situation (we are thinking of Renzo Novatore in Italy), Zo d'Axa effectively distanced himself from the anarchist movement while continuing to remain outside every herd. How much bitterness in the conclusion he reaches at the end of his story: "Here I am forced to conclude: I am not an anarchist". Surrounded by religious anarchists who were convinced of the necessity of the earthly Eden, the iconoclast Zo d'Axa came to deny his own anarchism. As if to say, if these are anarchists, I could not be one. A conclusion to which the anarchist movement might like to push many of its heretics even today. Later drawn to recuperate them, of course, when a century's distance is considered enough to neutralize their original subversive charge. It then becomes possible to dedicate highly sympathetic articles to them, like that of Charles Jacquier, taken from an official historical review of anarchism. It even becomes possible to give these heretics some retrospective display. There is still time to raise a statue to Zo d'Axa in the public square.

# FROM MAZAS
# TO JERUSALEM

*Chapter 1*

# MALEFACTOR

### The Arrest

IT ALL HAPPENED SO FAST. ONE THURSDAY IN APRIL — EIGHT days before May Day. At five in the morning, a long, loud ringing ringing in my home, a racket on the stairs, invasion of my lodging: it is a police search.

Papers and documents in the air, they look for weapons in the study; dishes and plates thrown everywhere with the pretext that the dining room cupboard hides dynamite.

In short, so as not to leave with empty hands, these gentlemen with a mission — there are twelve of them — snatch letters from friends, take possession of a few random manuscripts and select from among the publications those that have red covers.

Furthermore, the search is only the preamble. Then there is the arrest. We dash off in a carriage towards the holding prison.

The reception is quite typical. The police lead me to a glass kiosk where three uniformed guards scribble something on registers. We wait in a large room with walls of worked stone in front of the kiosk window. Suddenly, one of the guards, with a bloated face, raises his head with his kepi[1]* at an angle over his ear.

"Head down!" – he brusquely shouts at me. "For who?"

"Ah! So that's the way it is; we'll see about that. Into solitary confinement. On hard bread. Will you salute me?"

"Don't count on it."

"Take him away!" – he barks, prey to agitation in his leather mug.

We start well. Dampness drips from the walls of the cell in which I am locked up, the bed has no bed straw, the chair is filthy. I am forced to walk up and down in a ten foot space.

So it isn't a dream . I am in prison. I don't know what they want to charge me with, but it could only be something relating to our *L'Endehors*. The Magistrate's Court and the Court of Assizes are no longer enough; today, by kidnapping me, they hope to gag it. Coincidentally, its anniversary is coming up in the next few days.

I will celebrate it alone.

But let's take a few steps back. We haven't been tilting at windmills. The conflict has cleared the way, and some battles

---

1  A French military cap with a flat circular top and a nearly horizontal visor

were right on target. All the press was forced to intervene when we launched our protest in favor of a convict, the unfortunate Reyner, who due to cowardly rancor and judicial complicity, was imprisoned in the jail at Nou Island for more than eight years, as a punishment for a crime committed by two accomplices, a municipal councilor and a priest.

Earlier still, we acted in favor of youngsters, the children of imprisoned comrades. We couldn't leave these kids, whose parents had been mercilessly struck by society as rebels, to die of hunger. Our appeal was not in vain: even some beggars gave all their money, and those with literary or artistic reputations got involved in aiding the weakest.

My mind goes back over all of this, considering it necessary and not at all banal...

I also think of those unselfish comrades who fight at our sides on the front lines, the children of the bourgeoisie who could have gone blissfully through their lives and who instead have chosen to struggle for the Idea and for joy. I think of these deserters of the bourgeois past with their pen and their courage at the side of the oppressed. A kind of elation strikes me; at a time like this, it does me good to remember, and this prison apprenticeship matters little to me, so long as my comrades remain free and on the ball – as long as they await my return, as soon as possible.

## Brigand Tale

The sound of keys; the door opens. The investigating judge has sent for me.

Stairways, passageways, long corridors follow one after the other. A police officer acts as my guide. He takes tender care to put me in irons, perhaps so that I don't lose him in the maze. Still more stairways and corridors... we arrive in the cramped waiting room of the investigating judge. In front of us, a plaque announces: "M. Anquetil, magistrate".

We go in. What will he make up?

This personage is sunk in an armchair. He has an exhausted air. He makes a court clerk read me a long lampoon that accuses me of this crime: I am affiliated with a band of brigands.

At least I know how things stand. The idea is original. And since I don't bat an eyelash, Anquetil, mumbling, reprimands me:

"We have taken revolutionary journals and papers frome your house... We have proof."

"Really?"

"There is also a list – a list of addresses!"

With a triumphant air he places the list before my eyes. It is the list of the journal's subscribers!...

"A list of addresses," he insists, shaking his paper. "It's serious. Why deny it?"

"That is what I ask myself."

"Furthermore, your articles bode well; you have furnished confirmation there. We were merely waiting for the propitious moment. We will demonstrate your relationship with other persons involved. You sent money to the families of outlaws. It is conclusive. What do you respond?"

"Nothing."

Precisely nothing! Because it would be even more foolish, and this time in a ridiculous way, for you to offer yourself to such a joke, for you to believe that there is a residue of honesty in these shifty-eyed judges who interrogate... and judge you.

Nothing to say in response, nothing at all!

Because these individuals attack you on order, because your very responses – cleverly twisted – would give flesh to the prosecutor's closing speech.

"Here is the statement. Sign it."

"No."

"Guard, take the accused away."

And the judge gives the guard a piece of paper with this written on it:

"I, Anquetil, investigating judge of the Magistrate's Court, communicate and order all the agents of public safety to conduct to the Mazas prison for those awaiting trial:

Zo d'Axa, age 27, charges with 'association with brigands'."

## Mazas

I am brought to an entrance in front of which a paddy wagon is parked. A dozen poor, ragged devils join us. Indeed the van is for us. One by one, we're hoisted up, chained, and away it goes!

You only have to take a tiny journey on this vehicle with unknown suspensions, suffocated for a quarter hour without being able to change your position, forced into a cubby-hole, tossed about against walls riddled with holes with a few meager slots for ventilation; the briefest journey in a paddy wagon is enough to make you understand, once and for all, the image of the "salad drainer".

We arrive at nightfall. We are at Mazas. Heavy locked doors, sentries pacing back and forth, grayish stone walls, steps echoing in the distance: everything is of an oppressive sadness.

You proceed to the formalities of incarceration: surname, name, measurement of height, rough description of traits.

Then there is the search, or rather the complete stripping.

Everything you have on, clothes, underwear and personal objects are piled in a jumble on the tiled pavement where, with feet as bare as your legs and all the rest, you have to wait for a little while.

Pants of an uncertain gray, a short, ragged shirt, a jacket without buttons are thrown at you. You take back your shoes, and there you are, fitted out, while you witness the plundering of your belongings.

In that sinister place, surrounded by guards with grim appearance, in the uncertain glimmer of a light bulb, the human swarm around the clothes you were forced to take off makes the mind turn to some episode in the Bondy Forest.[2]

Darkness is the absolute ruler in the new cell in which I am then imprisoned.

Not even a crust of bread to end this eventful and exhausting day: he who sleeps has already dined!

I blindly sought my bed, and the effort granted me the gift of a heavy sleep until the next morning...

A bell rings.

It is the wake up call. Bunches of keys jangling. You hear the sound of the long row of cells opening one after the other. The sound approaches. A guard appears.

---

2   Bondy Forest, near Paris, was one the hunting terrain of thieves.

"Hey, number 9, on your feet! Where's your tin plate? Don't you want water?"

"But, of course."

"And your tin plate?" he repeats as he disappears, "if you don't want water, it means you'll have it tomorrow."

My jailer is pleased. In the end, I get up. The bed divides the cell crosswise. It is a barricade against circulation. It is likely that it is not supposed to stay that way during the day. This is confirmed for me almost immediately. The guard, stuffed into his green uniform, edged in yellow with brass buttons, dressed like a petty officer, reconfirmed it in a harsh tone when he appeared again:

"Come on! Fold up the covers, peel off the hammock... You're supposed to do it every morning at wake up call."

The cell is small but very bright from a harsh light that is reflected overhead. For furnishings, the famous tin plate, a covered wash tub, a massive table, a chair crudely stuffed with straw and attached to the table with an iron chain.

At the height of the spyhole made in the door, there is a small shelf on which the provisions that are passed from the outside are put. That is where they lay the black bread, not the fine bread of the military with the crispy, golden crust, but a damp, squishy bread, a bran loaf. Around nine, they bring a tin with a transparent liquid in which a slice of carrot floats. At three in the afternoon, the second and last meal: rice. It's whiteness is immaculate, the grains are fine and hard, and could bounce on the pavement. Maybe a fakir could enjoy it – I don't have the taste for that sort of buddhism.

But what is particularly painful is the tone with which you are scolded, at any time, inappropriately. It is the insolence of the galley sergeant. Twenty times a day a face appears at the peephole and grimly looks around:

"Clean up! There are bread crumbs on the floor. Open the window. Close the window. Give yourself something to do… instead of fantasizing about your filth!"

And twenty times a day, the little opening of the peephole is slammed shut again – like a slap in the face.

Could you ever imagine what a complete man, considered somewhat particular in life and forced to submit to every sort of tyranny in this place, might feel?

And yet, he is only warned.

It doesn't matter. There is no smoke without a roast, there is no imprisonment without a defect. Besides, when a judge abuses you with his suspicions, isn't it normal for the prison lackeys to overwhelm you with their exuberant contempt?

But it is precisely then, in that moment, that you urgently feel the need to stand most proudly. Your touchiness grows. You rebel. You answer back with arrogance. We require respect – but jail is what we get.

I have experienced it personally.

I will say that at times solitary confinement can be relaxing.

During the endless days, you come to detest the hard, implacable light on the white walls of the cell, a raw, cruel light.

In solitary, however, it is almost dark. Much better!

There is no bed, only a blanket. But you are spied on less, scolded less. It is a kind of dungeon. There you roll up in the blanket as if you were camping, and in the shadow, thought goes far away…

But the bread is hard.

And then? No, the most unbearable thing is not the material conditions. Rather, it's the contact with the noxious, taunting jailer. What a relief when evening falls, and this disagreeable individual goes from cell to cell for the last time, grunting:

"To bed. Go to sleep!"

Another day is over. Not the least bit entertaining. Still there was the walk, but it is quite a poor distraction.

Thirty minutes to walk around in a circular courtyard divided into compartments that branch out from a central turret from which the guard dominates every sector.

It is an open air cell.

To go there, you have to endure still more outrages. When the time comes, a guard shouts:

"Get ready!"

When the door is opened, you have to lie in wait and, quick, launch yourself. Quickly! Rapidly away from the cells. Like beasts driven into a hole. Toward the door there, which an arrogant guard half opens. More quickly! And the crazy line is in a trap. What a walk! Whose turn:

"Come on! Hurry! Hurry! For God's sake, come on..."

For me, all this just slowed my step.

## Interlude

You'd have reason to feel sorry for yourself, if you had the romantic tendency to dramatize. The reality is enough and more. Without a doubt, you become a victim. We agree, prison existence is vile. But I have to admit, you maintain a happy turn of mind that allows you to hear when a merry note sounds. So in the course of the search an incident took place that seemed to me like an interlude.

I had already taken my clothes off and the crouching cops were going through the pockets. Suddenly one of them dropped my jacket and let out a shout.

"Something moved, there!"

"Come on!"

"I tell you, something moved!"

There was a panic: a bomb, and explosive, an incendiary device[3]! A silence over which terror hung; you could have heard a wick burning...

Still, the most determined of the guards, like a heroic slave to duty, came forward, and taking a thousand and one precautions, he picked the jacket back up. Each movement was measured, calculated, analyzed, subtle, soft if I dare say so.

He fingered the jacket in slow motion, scanning the lining. He slid his hand into a pocket and, turning his head a bit, pulled a body out of that appeared to be wiggling – humbly hidden among lettuce leaves. It was only a turtle.

"Ah! So that's what it is."

"We will have to inform the corporal."

But right away, there's another problem. The corporal doesn't want to assume responsibility for the decision. Consider! What are they supposed to do – they had not

---

3 The French here is "marmite à renversement", which seems to literally mean a pot that has been spilled, but in the Italian from which I translated this, they used "ordigno", device. Perhaps this was French slang for such a thing at the time. Or perhaps Zo d'Axa was being sarcastic, and the English phrase "a tempest in a teapot" would fit his intention.

foreseen the situation – what is supposed to be done with the animal? A difficult question.

The scene goes on and on and becomes grotesque. In the middle of the double line of cells, the group of uniformed men are gesticulating around a small turtle.

The head guard rushes in. He investigates, weighs things up and makes his judgment.

"Where is the beast?"

"There, there," every tense finger points.

"Smash that disgusting thing in the locker room."

Pellison had even less luck with his famous girlfriend. Certain details amuse me, but the small nuances they evoke don't just make me smile. Couldn't the indifferent furnishings on which I myself now lounge be the rudimentary accommodations of the most skeptical of my readers tomorrow? The prison hospitality at Mazas is eclectic: the whole world is at the mercy of the judge's whims. Without a shadow of doubt, these tiny incidents, told as they present themselves, offer the specific flavor of what will follow! Poor turtle! Furthermore, it is pretty in its warm ochre shell decorated with hexagons fringed in black. I had thought that, by bringing it, I would be able to break the monotonous immobility of things during my time in prison. A disappointed hope. A few days later, the corporal of the guards, an old man with a gray mustache, comes to me scowling:

"Your beast made a hell of a racket in the locker room."

The same day, a gentleman with a three-striped kepi, but a fatherly appearance, is making the round of inspections.

This gentleman is the warden.

He explains to me that he loves animals. The turtle will be given to someone outside.

"Why can't it be left in my cell?"
"It would die there…"
"How?"
"From the lack of air, of course."

## In Solitary Confinement

In the silence of the locked cell, you feel time slip by second by second, grain upon grain like in an hourglass.

This has already gone on for three weeks, with no news from the outside, no visits from dear friends. Family and friends knock at Mazas' heavy doors in vain. Even if I had wanted to defend myself legally, I wouldn't have been able to. What they grant almost immediately to the most compromised defendants, they tenaciously refuse to me. I have no right to a lawyer. I am vegetating, cut off from the outside world. Confinement is mandatory, the interest of the inquiry demands it:

I am in solitary confinement!

And the nerve-racking comedy continues. What is more, as to the inquiry, they haven't even attempted a second interrogation.

They aren't worried about hiding how arbitrary my imprisonment is. Why bother themselves about it, and for whom?

Each day that comes is worse than the last.

From daybreak, when the wake-up call throws you off your cot, until nightfall, which comes so slowly, there are feet coming and going, pawing the ground as in a cage.

Four measured steps in one direction, about face, and four measured steps in the other direction; this becomes a tyrannical habit. Obsessions take possession of you: your feet always land in the same place, turning with the usual abrupt movement. Again and again, too many of those turns.

No desire to sit down at the table to write; a vague uncertainty fashions floating visions; you follow them with a fateful step, far and wide, with dangling arms.

You wait for something without knowing precisely what, but something new. It can't be long now. Some communication is imminent. Right now?

You stop with a jolt.

Your eye looks at the door; your ear listens attentively. Still nothing.

You start the merry-go-round again: four steps, face to the wall, about face...

Perhaps this wears out the need for physical activity. Perhaps the desire to speed up the slow hours is deceived by traversing more space.

The moments don't inflict themselves any less as stagnant eras.

Days seem like they will never end. This sort of feverish vigilance, still in the lively one, sharps the senses in a singular way. Hearing acquires a particular acuity. You can distinguish the comings and goings of this or that guard, of an officer or of the warden.

Because the warden has the coquettish idea to visit the cells often. He comes in with a suave, deceptively good-natured, inquisitive air. He knows that isolation and a long deprivation of speech makes less talkative folks loquacious, so he readily takes on the role of a spy.

He enjoys it.

Once it was my turn to tell him what I thought of the prison regime.

Such a fine thing, imprisonment!

Made to cure them, isn't it? The malefactors, they're sick.

Well then, let's stop to examine this social therapy, this cure for defectives. Abandoned to obsession, man bleeds his life away. Many don't bear up under the torments of preventive detention. Every day, someone has to be taken down from the bars where he is dangling, his throat close by a strip of his shirt. Sometimes they are innocent.

Solitary confinement consumes energy.

Prison is perverted. Other men collapse slowly. They call up their dearest memories to escape the present. Character harden, the minds breaks down, taken over by carnal yearnings that burn in solitude. Would you try to tell me that you aren't aware of the writings that stain the walls, all the confessions incised with nails, those revealing confessions?

Tidy stuff. this prison work!

From my first words, I noticed that my questioner, the chief tormentor of eleven hundred prisoners, found it difficult to hide a dull irritation, but he quickly composed himself, resuming his suave attitude, and with a wink:

"I understand," he told me, "Above all else, I am a humanitarian."

I had opportunities to verify his touching humanitarianism. He showed it at his leisure in small things. I noticed it when I was suffering so badly that I couldn't drag myself to the infirmary and they left me without any care in order to save the doctor the trouble of coming.

They replaced the doctor with a nurse – this seemed to

be customary – who treated the fever by drowning it in herbal tea.

According to this paternal administration, there is nothing better than licorice water.

The best of it is that, in this instance, this panacea worked for me.

So I won't linger over this any more, since I am in a considerable hurry to get to matters that should keep the attention much more lively. Regulation, hateful in itself, is aggravated in practice by petty cruelty.

Repression stinks of vengeance.

Even when it isn't the order of the day, it is at least permitted. Prisoners are abandoned to the insensitivity of the jailers who consider it their duty to hate.

It was in this model-prison as well, in roughly the same time-frame, that a young prisoner who was coughing too much was given a radical cure. He was taken to the shower and rinsed down with icy water.

According to the guards, this was the hydro-therapeutic method!

I am not making anything up; I am just stating the facts. I am not the only one who knows what happened.

There is a crying mother.

The murder victim was named Chabard – he was seventeen years old.


## "Comrade" Cop

One morning, they informed me that I had to get ready to go to the anthropometric department.

Malefactors have to get measured!

I don't give them any problems because I want to see the laboratory of the notorious Dr. Bertillon. At nine, I am taken to the police station in a paddy wagon. In a back room, a corporal shouts out names. The prisoners respond one after the other. They don't at all have the appearance that is usually attributed to the habitual frequenters of the fatherland's jails. They go forward proudly with a light, quiet, almost scornful step. But I am not mistaken; most of these prisoners are simple revolutionaries. They are propagandists who were definitely not caught with lock-picks in hand.

We quickly exchange a few words. The latest prisoners tell the news. All three of the newspapers that form the indomitable small press in Paris have been targeted.

The same treatment as *L'Endehors* received.

The editors of *Révolte* and *Père Peinard* are under arrest.[4*]

Also arrested: public speakers, men of action and a bout sixty random individuals described as dangerous in police reports.

Those here do not all share the same ideas or underlying reasons, so much less the same confidence in the future. Nonetheless, they have a common, disinterested tendency toward the best. And here it is, the association!

I don't know all my accomplices, but I love them.

After whole days spent alone with jailers, you are glad to finally find yourself again among human beings.

What will they try to do to us?

Some have already considered the idea that we might be moved in mass to Guiana or Nouvelle. The government that

---

4  Jean Grave and Emile Pouget, respectively.

links us to professional assassins is capable of anything. Still, we will deny them the satisfaction of mocking our attitude.

Together now, we feel solidarity; we defy fate.

The spirit is contagious. The corporal no longer gets the silence he demands. He yells. He roars uselessly. The gravity of the situation and the solemnity of the place decidedly do not disturb us.

And the roll call goes on amidst a festive brouhaha...

A police invasion, as many guards as there are we men. Quickly they handcuff us, and no one protests; we accept things cheerfully:

"Goodbye, see you later."

We go in line, single-file, but sufficiently separated, through the endless corridors of the building with arched ceilings – like a catacomb. The procession gets longer, but not at all gloomy.

At one turn, the guard walking in front of me leaves his prisoner, turns around and talks to his colleague.

"Leave this one to me; let's change."

The colleague accepts and abandons me to the newcomer. Well, what does this cop want from me? Does he intend to make me feel the chains of the handcuffs more? He is a young man, about thirty years old, very dark, with a frank air:

"I wanted to tell you," he says in a low voice, "that Very, the cabaret Very, was attacked Monday evening."[5*]

---

5  Lherot, a waiter at the Very restaurant who was unharmed by the explosion of April 25, 1892, would accuse Ravachol. Consequently, he hid out as a prison guard in the central prison of Melun in order to escape reprisal.

And the cop starts to shake my hand in a rare outpouring: "Yes," he told me, "I am a comrade!"

In the meantime we have reached the front of the line. They make us enter in groups of ten into a basic locker room with benches and coat racks. A single guard follows us. He isn't mine.

The innovator Bertillon appears, surrounded by his assistants.

"Take your clothes off; feet bare. Keep only the shirt and pants."

We go into the hot room. Is there anything they don't measure? A few tools and calipers are supposed to allow these specialists to measure people and their value. The width of my cranium is known almost to the millimeter. They know my height, standing and sitting, the size of my right ear and the length of my left foot. And many other things as well.

While measuring my forefinger, an employee deigns to inform me: they are defending society here.

Perhaps the only gap is that they don't note the measure of the shrug.

"No tattoos?"

The details are marked on a list. The list ends up in a filing cabinet. It will be completed shortly with a photograph. Once they have passed through here, repeat offenders can no longer deny their identity. This is the most obvious advantage. But there are others as well:

Mr. Bertillon does quite a bit of business.

In exchange for a bit of advertising, this gentleman gives the newspapers pictures of famous murderers and allows their sale to amateurs for a high price.

Even though today he is dealing with modest personalities who won't draw many requests, and even though he imposes a humiliating inquisition on us, at least, Mr. Bertillon, the man-measurer will expand his own collection.

On a higher floor, in front of the photographic laboratory where the small museum is set up, we are placed in line for the pose. I notice innocent affectations: hands combing through the waves of the hairiest manes.

The laboratory is connected to the room of anthropometric revelations by means of a narrow staircase. We are left without surveillance and start gabbing again.

I tell the others about the explosion on Magenta Boulevard.

It is like a balm for the consciousness – a cry of triumph. However, no one seems to be bloodthirsty here. But the information is ennobled by the celebration it called forth. This response of unprecedented audacity, readily foreseeable and bursting forth in its time, despite all the surveillance and the arrests, reveals a latent potential and implacable wills. The men are stirred to enthusiasm.

In the midst of this ferment, I tell them how I came to find out. I talk about the3 cop who confessed to me:

"I am a comrade – the comrade of rebels."

So there are comrades even in the army of repression.

Will it end with talk of conspiracy? It gets better. An idea moves forward and makes way everywhere.

## **Little Details Behind the Scenes**

The police raid of April 1892 will be historic.

Chronologically, it was the first of the most cynical attacks of the times against freedom of thought.

Today we know the hidden details of the event.

The government had decided to take advantage of the emotions evoked by the explosions at the Lobau barracks and at rue de Clichy by intentionally including all active revolutionaries in a huge trial. The ministry and its docile prosecutors claimed that certain ideas constituted complicity. The writer who explained how so many of the disinherited are inevitably drawn to theft himself became a thief simply because he expressed these thoughts. The thinker who examined the reasons for "propaganda by the deed" became the secret accomplice of the one who lit the tragic fuse.

The philosopher no longer ha the right to declare his indulgence and consider events without getting dizzy.

Society wanted to rid itself of those of its members depraved enough to want to better it.

The reactionary rulers could have finally enjoyed themselves in tranquility and let their remorse slumber for a long time – since at least their doubts would no longer be roused by the words of killjoys.

They chose the moment with skill.

Dynamite attacks had terrorized the capitalist bourgeoisie, more fearful perhaps for their real estate than for themselves. It was on the eve of the ominous demonstrations of May. They were afraid. And the cowardly crowd would all surely have applauded summary executions.

The raid took place.

Aimed particularly against the anarchist struggle, nonetheless, the arrests also came down on individuals whose independence was such that they refused any label – including that of anarchist. So, I was arrested, even though I had never set foot in a public meeting or visited any group. Even though I had always affirmed my lack of involvement in sects and schools, *L'Endehors*, outsider, that is to say, by myself, researcher of the beyond, fomenter of ideas, it made no difference. Irreverence, if it was truly combative, was enough. All ferment had to be smothered. One malefactor less – I was collared.

Treacherously carried out, the event was disguised with a legal appearance. The legal code is so elastic that they claimed that they were applying articles 265 and following concerning criminal association to us:

"Article 266. This crime consists in the sole offence of the organization of a gang or a link between gangs and their leaders or commanders, or of agreements made to justify, distribute or divide up the product of misdeeds."

Now do you understand the investigating judge's insinuations about the "address list" and the "dispatch of money"?

"Article 267. When this crime is not accompanied by any other, the creators, the directors of the association, and the leading commanders and subordinates of such gangs, will be punished with temporary forced labor."

A pleasant prospect of slave labor opens before us.

It was obvious that we couldn't count on the impartiality of the judges. The word of command was given. We'd have a lovely time proving that not only were we not pickpockets, but there was no organization of any sort among us – not even from a political point of view. The courts would have struck us with equal ease.

Only one point was argued. For the operation to succeed, it seems that other countries would have had to have similar trials against their refractory citizens.

Well, what the French republic had premeditated, the Netherlands, England and Germany had the decency to refuse. The ancient monarchies didn't give in to the incitements of the young republic that dreamed of reconstituting the international in the opposite sense. There were negotiations that led nowhere. The hunt against free men was not decreed throughout Europe. Our collapsing democracy then felt that they couldn't prove itself to be worse than the worst autocrats.

The opportunistic government hesitated, lost its composure like a badly trained scoundrel – and didn't dare to go on to the very end.

That day it said: it will happen some other time!

## Provisional Liberty

After Bertillon's offensive measurements, we would go back to Mazas – but only for a few days.

The release order came.

The politicao-judiciary machinations failed miserably. They were barely able to keep us in prison for a month and could no longer injure our wrists with their despicable handcuffs...

It wasn't much. The predatory magistrates, whose orders the government had changed, expressed their vexation in a singular fashion. Obliged to release us, the investigating judges took great care not to issue an order of "no place to proceed". It seemed best to them to still leave room for doubt, to keep a threat hanging over our heads. They adopted a half-measure – faithfully following the letter of the release orders; they simply agreed to put us on "provisional liberty".

A clever trick.

An order of "no place to proceed" would have been a frank public confession that there were no grounds for the charges.

Belated confessions are repugnant to judges.

This horror for confession is as visibly entrenched among judges as it is in their pitiful caseload of shameful defendants.

Furthermore, don't we find a further point in common? Spending so much time together, they end up vaguely resembling one another.

Who has not witnessed the hearings of ribald court president, a keen connoisseur of morals trials, a scrutinizer, undressing details? Or the shifty-eyed judge's aide who knows it all, who is an authority on shady deals? Or the prosecutor, that fine young man, who pushes his cap to the side with a mocking movement of the hand borrowed from a sidewalk d'Artagnon?

Repeat offenders and executioners imitate, renew and complete each other.

Avinain's motto remains a program for pretenders who perpetrate judicial errors, blunders and crimes: never confess!

Mr. Anquetil, my judge, Anquetil-Avinain, qualified enough to honor his guild, cunning though awkward – a jack of all trades, he behaved like a good judge – he confessed nothing.

This sycophant of power, greedy for bonuses, told himself to take account of his imaginative zeal: by applying the half measure of provisional liberty, appearances would be saved.

Ambiguity would be prolonged...

What does it matter! It was secondary. Mazas opened its doors again. And on a mild May evening, I resumed my place in life. The sound of the street is beautiful. Generally, I didn't listen to it, although I always heard it. It is a strong, sweet, penetrating harmony, in which tireless activity vibrates, in which love sings.

The prison comrades, the anarchists, came out arm in arm, exuberant, mocking the prison walls.

Long live provisional liberty! The term did not scare us. We know the danger of our poor freedom well – it is always provisional. It is a crime to desire to be yourself and strive to free yourself. It is an arrogance for which you pay. It is forbidden to think out loud. It is forbidden to speak of life as affected by the sensations. This is the crime. I am proof of it, I who am nothing, I who don't want to be anything, I who go my way alone...

*Chapter 2*

# INCITEMENT TO MURDER

## Forward in Case of Absence

Ravachol's noisy innovations only cracked a few buildings, but caused many cracks in the balding skulls of our rulers.

The latter – it's the perfect opportunity to say it – these scum, had carried out arbitrary arrests. Though seized with panic, still they had not deceived themselves. They knew quite well that in the end they would end up releasing men against whom, when all is said and done, they could articulate nothing. But they told themselves:

"Mazas will tranquilize them!"

But Mazas didn't tranquilize a thing.

You would have to have the mentality of a clumsy grafter to think that prison is a decisive argument.

If certain of our ministers have manifested an edifying repentance, the repentance of being made to own up, after being forced to give up the check books taken from banks to the clerk of the court, hefty sums that, besides, the administration is quite happy to politely conceal until their departure – what does that prove?

It wouldn't be logical for honest young men, thrown into prison without explanation or reason, to declare themselves satisfied at the end of months of preventive detention and to come out of Mazas shouting, "Long live the justice system!"

Indeed, precisely the opposite occurred.

Their lives interrupted, their affairs disturbed, their means of subsistence frequently lost, the victims of these provocative raids come out of prison more rebellious than when they went in.

It is not going too far to point to the pimps of power as inherent enemies.

At home, the little ones go hungry, the baker refuses to give credit, the landlord talks about selling, the boss has replaced you.

Rage grows.

It boils over. At this point some impulse might drive you to kill yourself.

And certainly the least determined move forward. The timid take courage.

In the reflective solitude of the cell, you trace the causes, you figure out who is responsible.

Ideas sharpen.

The individual, imprisoned for the platonic crime of subversive social love, learns to hate.

Around him, friends, neighbors, workmates, witnesses to unjustified abuses, understand, develop and swell the numbers of the discontented – irreconcilable tomorrow. And the outcome is the ferment of minds. Agitation. It is a beautiful, propagating reflex.

Imprisonment is never useless. Even when unjustly fired workers are not involved. Even when the person struck is someone for whom the pen is a tool and a weapon. It is so obvious. Repression is stimulating. It drives away the final reservations. It burns its bridges behind it. It sharpens the desire for revenge.

Full of life and particularly vivacious, I go back to my journal. The prosecution against me and the attempt to strangle *L'Endehors* were the opportunity for fierce personalities to express themselves courageously, and they did, in the same place where I had battled each week. The ridiculous charges had thus brought me new collaborators and provided encouraging evidence of a promising solidarity for the future. I could only take cheer in my sojourn in Mazas.

So much the more because the work in which I took pride was two-fold. It wasn't only about the social debates that I have barely started – and will see tomorrow; I also intended to create a robust group of young people to include in the next campaign. I wanted to give a free journal to the writers of the time, thirsty like me for straightforward language, a platform where they could express their thoughts completely. I wanted the first realization of this ideal grouping, without hierarchy, without bit-players, in which the individual, the artist, would be able to make his full personality blossom while still ensuring that he cannot be labeled at all. This was *L'Endehors*.

And our journal of blistering attack rushed off with the contrary wind, defying the reefs. Shall I name the crew? It would be a nearly complete list of the young generation of thinkers – the bold! We will probably find them still together, these passionate talents – all these men. And what winning contributions they could make to a daily paper!...

The cash?

Perhaps we'd get it.

If I didn't regret having known Mazas, I would owe special thanks to the trio that had me locked up: the massive minister, Loubet, inspired by Quesnay de Beaurepaire, who has the honor of having invented the offense of criminal association, with Anquetil as accomplice.

So I called my first article "Three Lackeys" and dedicated it to these gentlemen.

Naturally the article contained certain reflections meant to show that the prison regime had not substantially changed my ideas.

The public prosecutor's office was curious to see how far I would push my stubbornness. The new case was an order to appear at the criminal court on the pretext of incitement to murder.

Whose murder? The three, so it seems. And this beats everything. Here is the phrase, or rather the witticism that so easily earned me eighteen months in prison:

"These people are from the same family. They must be from the same branch – the branch from which ropes with slip knots hang."

I quote this as a point of information, just like other newspapers at the time, and furthermore I prudently add that I implore the population to resist any mad urge that might assail them if, because they read this, they were tempted to rush in mass into the parkway of the court to hang the designated personages from a sycamore tree.

Eighteen months in prison!

And a three thousand franc fine as well! But what am I saying? Three thousand? No, six thousand.

And not eighteen months, but thirty-six! Because they weren't content with taking such action against me; they also struck the good and unselfish managing editor, Matha, who hadn't even read the article, with the same punishment.

Poor Matha. Wouldn't someone later accuse him of robbing the villas in Ficquefleur and blowing up Parisian restaurants?

They wanted to get rid of *L'Endehors* at all costs – but we'd be the ones to pay those costs.

They intended to break up a suspicious group, cooling the enthusiasm, imposing silence, extinguishing a fire.

It was a light breeze on the fire.

Besides, I wisely took care not to handle anything any more, and cynically decided to avoid police attention. I had a good reason for this, aside from my love of freedom: the very life of my journal.

Not to mention the charm of doing and saying what I please without restrictions.

When the hearing ended, while still under the influence of the judicial farce, I fired off my parting shot.[6] The pages

---

[6] I use the phrase as known in English, but in the French the term is

I wrote at the time would play an incidental part in earning me new prosecutions. But first I had the intense pleasure of formulating without reservation and clarifying to my taste a certain red hot remedy.

The second article was entitled "Lhérot de Beaurepaire", two names that match up well in shameful harmony, a synthesis of these times, filthy with arrogance and snitching. And while the censure of finicky judges underlined the many incriminating passages with colored pencil, making the page look like a multi-colored flag, I was packing my bags to leave – strongly seduced by the prospect of remaining outside of prison, shooting sharp darts.

With comrades, of course.

Emile Henry, whose constant concern was to work for an idea, took charge, without pay, of the annoying chores of administration, correspondence with distributors, and mailing out *L'Endehors*.

As modest and ordinary as these tasks were, he wanted to collaborate in the common work. He did it even though we had our differences: but doesn't anarchy have a close kinship to my individualistic conception that affirms pride in being outside of narrow rules, outside of the constrictions of the law?

I still hear him, barely more than a child, and yet already so serious. Concentrated, even sectarian, as those

---

actually *flèche du Parthe*, that is, Parthian arrow. It is a reference to the Parthians, an ancient population of northeastern Iran, who would shoot arrows in simulation of retreat before the enemy, and then take them by surprise. The term Parthian, or parting, shot now refers to a biting comment launched at the end of a conversation. – translator whose faith is no longer disturbed by doubt necessarily become; they see the goal – I want to say, they are nearly hypnotized – and then reason, judge, condemn with a mathematical implacability. He firmly believed in the coming of a future society, logically built and harmoniously beautiful.

The thing that he chided me for was that I didn't counting enough on human regeneration, didn't compare everything to the anarchist ideal. Apparent contradictions shocked his logic. He was astonished that one who understood the baseness of the times could still find some joy there.

The will to live! And I might add: immediately! Individual emancipation. And struggle for the pleasure of struggle and of disrespect. Contagious, even fruitful, example. In any case: to live! Recalcitrants, not dupes – not even of the future. Beyond distant hopes …

Weren't these hopes what he wanted to die for?

Another dedicated friend, Etienne Decrept, took on the responsibilities of editorial administration. His devotion and courage were probably the reason that, at the time of the latest raids, he became a wanted man.

In fact, the relentlessness of the men of justice had not taken a break. We had to go through it all, at least everything that was possible. And is it over? You know about Alexander Cohen's expulsion. You recall what the minister said when Emile Zola asked about the reasons that drove him to chase a laborer and scholar out of France.

"The collection of *L'Endehors* was seized from Cohen."

He did collaborate with us – with a short story translated from Malayan!

And didn't they bring this infamous collection of *L'Endehors* up everywhere, even in the substantial evidence in the Vaillant trial? And yet, had he read and understood us, this desperate man who – wanting to strike and die – only struck half-way?

Felix Fénéon's crime was more serious: aside from the artistic colored notes that he dared to sign on our pages, after my departure, he willingly talked about the paper at times with audacious malefactors like Lucien Descaves, Pierre Quillard, Hérold, Bernard Lazare, Barrucand or Mirbeau who collaborated on articles. How is it possible to imagine the recklessness of this employee of the ministry of war who allowed himself not only to be a keen art critic, but also to remain a faithful friend through hard times?

The tasks that I had accumulated more or less diligently, in my free time, were distributed. Nothing more remained for me to do but to send in good copy; I wouldn't fail.

The police tailed me.

I received the order to turn myself in. The commissioner in charge, Clément, called me to come to his office to deal with new legal proceedings.

I preferred London.

Just as well that the papers from Clément would arrive for me by post stamped:

"FORWARD IN CASE OF ABSENCE".

*Chapter 3*
# ENGLISH HOLIDAY

### Tit for Tat

When you are presented with an invitation that is not properly formulated, it is correct to excuse yourself. When a disreputable person makes this invitation, it is best to decline the offer with a few courteous words. And this is why today I take up my pen with the intention of making an amicable response to the following love letter[7] that the police administration sent to me:

"By virtue of the instructions from the Public Prosecutor, I have the honor of requesting your presence in my chambers."

This fine note is signed "Clément."

---

7  The French word here is *poulet*. It literally translates as "chicken," but is used in slang both for a love letter and as an insulting term for a cop.

Is it about lunch, an interrogation, or an attempt to hire me? I don't even want to think about it. If I refuse the brief visit, it is only because I have taken advantage of the beautiful weather and am on holiday far away from the Seine riverbanks of the Goldsmiths.[8]

Oh! The absorbing tranquility of vacations! Mr. de Beaurepaire, you who hole up in the countryside leaving phony addresses, who might understand better than you:

"So I don't want any of it, dear count, and all to you."

As to the subordinate Clément, who sought the appointment on behalf of his boss Quesnay, he wouldn't expect a personal response. He tries to be gracious without success, but it is hard to carry on a correspondence through the servants. It is enough to write to the boss.

One needs to recognize that the commissioners and deputies, the Cléments, like the Croupis, the Anquetils or the Couturiers, only have a relative responsibility. All the abuses of power, all the vile acts, that constitute their daily tasks, are assigned to them precisely by the pseudo-nobility in charge of state vengeance. They are merely the most humble slaves who never ask questions. It's in their blood. Predestined to servitude and kicks in the ass, they could have been buffoons at a fair—instead they are court magistrates.

Quesnay, the director of the ill-famed building in which they serve, provides work, assigns rooms, while the girlishly-robed magistrates trot back and forth through the halls of the Palace of Justice.

---

[8] *Quai des Orfèvres*, office of the *Sûreté*, the French police

It is curious that, despite the sound organization, capable of causing months of prison and thousands of francs in fines to rain down as thick as hail, they always come up with new trials.

The young men of the times who talk of freedom throw the weaklings in power into such a panic that they completely lose their heads. They tremble and don't even try to hide it.

Now they want to change the law about the press.

It's just that the deputies in charge of studying the question are faced with a serious difficulty. They agree about striking at persistently rebellious writers, but they are afraid that as a side-effect they would harm the pen-pushers, their brothers, from monarchists to radicals, who break their lances for show in the great departmental debates.

This, this is sacred…

So come on! The heritage of our fathers… the sacred conquests of our glorious ancestors… the children of 1789 don't want them brought into question.

So they came up with a little plan full of leniency for crimes against the security of the state, They are legitimate, those ones there. That is part of the heritage.

The politicians will be able to continue their games.

Only attacks against the principle of authority will be suppressed.

At least the revolutionaries will know which of their weapons of attack are most feared. The Commission of honorable men has pointed them out:

Instigation to murder, theft and dynamite attacks.

Blood, gold and destruction. And if it were true?…

And was this law on the press really well envisioned?

It even mentions incitement to disobedience addressed to soldiers.

Would the tactic emerge like this? The horizon broadened, the horizon where one glimpses rifle butts raised, like a moving forest?

It would be childish to worry about the increase in penalties.

In the future, one will evade preventative arrest with the same casual ease with which one avoids appointments and ambushes today.

Rebels are not still living in 1830 as they would like to believe. Romanticism has had its time and then some. They can no longer fool anyone with such crude traps. They will have to reckon on incorrigibles who know the subtleties of conflict.

Still the alarm of the people of position is a good symptom.

We will respond tit for tat—without useless sacrifice, without boastful harangues. Very alert. Very self-confident.

The gentlemen of the parliament can fabricate exceptional laws as they please.

The gray Terror makes us laugh.

## Socialist Babel

I have been living in London for far too short a time to be able to say politely just how tiresome I think it all is. You live by impressions, and perhaps here it is best to shut up. But isn't it a stroke of bad luck to find yourself right in the middle of a socialist conference?

## English Holiday

Of course, this wasn't deliberate. I went out for a walk in the city with no bad intentions, when a comrade I met dragged me into the lobby of the Westminster where the miners' delegates were giving a series of presentations. There were not only Englishmen there, but also Germans, Frenchmen and Belgians. It was the international meeting of foremen.

Only one of them wore a worker's smock without posing—but also without weakness… It was Thivrier[9]!

A superb site.

The Germans were stern, the Belgians were good children, the English were quite distinguished, and the French were frauds.

An imposing show! And one that will remain forever engraved in the memories of those who were allowed to follow the debate from the height of the three large public galleries—indeed, there were thirteen of us.

Besides, the number doesn't mean much: representative Vaillant was among us as well as Mrs. Aveling Marx, who supervised the distribution of the leaflets, advertising the works of the late Karl, during the intermission.

We weren't bored for even a second. They spoke in vague terms about the eight-hour day and the general strike. They nominated officers and made the vigorous decision to meet again next year to discuss urgent questions.

I kid you not.

---

[9] Christophe Thivrier, a republican socialist in France, best known for being the world's first socialist mayor (1882 in Commentry, France). He was elected to the French National Assembly—a house of the French Parliament—in 1889.

They decided on nothing, nothing at all. By the last day, they hadn't even reached an agreement on the best way to vote.

When the time came for parting, the sixty-two English delegates still claimed that voting took place by delegates, while the eight Belgians, the four Germans and the four Frenchmen maintained with more vigor that it was necessary to vote by country.

It was socialist Babel.

It wasn't just a confusion of tongues that reigned, but a confusion of intelligence.

Parliamentary quibbling created the sole, phony basis for understanding.

The general interests of the miners should have led to unanimous resolutions of conflict; instead these socialists preferred petty national factions that sowed discord and turned comrades into enemies.

This endless discussion on the method of voting sometimes even threatened to make the debate a bit dull; and that was when one could appreciate the advantages of French fury: the delegate Lamendaim, from Pas-de-Calais, let out a howl. His colleague Calvignac, from Marseilles, banged his fist on the table, pretending to go into a rage. It was irresistible. The whole room writhed.

Yes, of course, you have to recognize, there was a good mood and spirit; they laughed a lot in the great room of Westminster. Quite a lot amused them during these chats, while down below, at the bottom of the gloomy pits, in dark tunnels, the firedamp awakens from the ceaseless blows of the mine tramps' pickaxes.

## English Holiday

However, the cheerful empirical legionnaires[10] at the conference had a brilliant idea: these people whose humble ideal consists in demanding eight hours of work, eight hours of independence and eight hours of sleep, these helmeted knights of the 3—8 understood that the delegates could, in their turn, carry the question before the parliament.

These brave conventioneers said: "Since it's the hour of battle, we can certainly discuss it."

Professional delegates have a marked propensity for honest means. In this case, they expressed the hope of achieving the goal "through parliamentary means."

At bottom, this is a viewpoint completely in keeping with conferences—paid vacations...

And when they don't make promises, these good, practical people formulate motions or loudly proclaim platonic evidence of their sympathy.

Always ostentatious.

"We are quite aware," said Lamendaim, "that the three hundred franc donation we are giving to the thousands of English strikers at Durham is a miserably small contribution, but it is proof of our solidarity. And this is enough."

The Belgians follow in line:

---

10 The French here reads: "Les joyeux empiriques". "Joyeux" usually means cheerful, but it is also a slang term for someone who has been sentenced to serve in the French foreign legion. Since there is no other noun in the clause, I suspect that Zo d'Axa intends this as a wordplay on the apparent good spirits just mentioned, but also on the fact that these delegates are all required by their various parties to be at this conference, just as legionnaires are required to serve in the hot deserts of North Africa.

"We have refrained," a Fleming declares, "not daring to make such a small offer. Three hundred francs is not much; still, I declare that we will send this amount without fail. All our brothers will know it."

After the Belgians, the Germans. Each does his part. The conference is coming to an end, and they prove their kindness:

They invite everyone to dinner.

As for the general strike, it seem that it will have to stay in the mist. They want to talk about it, not do it. The solution would be too energetic. And it would bring the entertainment to a close.

It's a question of negotiating, not acting.

The sword of Damocles of authoritarian socialists will keep hanging for a long time.

Though ordinarily they talk with difficulty, these gentlemen are, above all, speakers—after-dinner speakers.

The exploiters of the miners, the capitalists, can sleep peacefully—for some time still. The attack will not come from this side. Real rebels are men of action. They reveal themselves when they strike.

When the dark slaves, stooping in the underground tunnels, rise up… and they want to … they will not ask the little Lamendaims for advice.

Fiercely and spontaneously, they will rise up—with axes and picks blazing in the sun.

So we leave the good conventioneers behind. They are still afraid of conflict. The easy life makes them bourgeois. They are mere dilettantes who travel around Europe as pontificating tourists: last year in Paris, today in London, next year they will land in Brussels.

Thivrier's smock is a dust rag!

## **The Melville Gang**

Judges generally abuse children's bodies. Most of the time it's like Rabaroust; but sometimes it is by pouring out the hypocrisy of their tears over babies that rebels' dynamite may "perhaps" strike in their cradles.

Meanwhile—and in this case not "perhaps" but certainly—they are the ones killing babies. They are the ones who, with the complicity of the police, throw the fathers into prison, pursue and torture the mothers and poison the milk of the newborn babies.

And this down-to-earth truth which no great phrase could explain will only amuse boorish brutes. This is a fact. The body of a child that we buried yesterday is again a sinister witness to it.

You remember the searches carried out in London against the comrade Delbecque with the aim of finding Francis and Meunier, accused of being the perpetrators of the Very good[11] dance party.

The police fiasco filled the cops' hearts with rage.

And for Delbecque and his female companion, there was a long series of persecutions of all sorts. The man was continually shadowed by police agents, harassed even in his laboratory, hounded around the people who gave him work and risked losing every job. The woman, who nursed a five-month-old kid at the time, became the target of the most odious plots: as soon as they knew she was alone, the investigators would

---

11 This is another reference to the attack against the Very cabaret mentioned in chapter 1. Zo d'Axa would add the English word "good" to Very when referring to this event.

wrangle their way into her house, passing on false news about her husband, sowing anxiety, trying to extort some compromising confession out of her through intimidation, forcefully offering this deal: tranquility at the price of informing. And since the women maintained her silence in dignity or raised her voice to hurl her contempt in the face of her tormentors, they turned it into a brutal, ongoing obsession. The mother's health didn't hold up against the moral tortures and her milk could no longer nourish the baby girl—causing her to die in slow agony.

At the time of the fruitless search, the exhausted bloodhounds felt excessively whipped by the irony of revolutionaries, an irony that was sometimes loud, even musical, since the retreat of the police was depicted by the sound of the hurdy-gurdy. So they told themselves: he who laughs last, laughs best.

They won the second round:

They laughed in front of a coffin.

And this isn't a lot of hot air. It isn't just an image.

They were seen.

On that gray September afternoon, as the funeral car waited at the front door of the house in mourning, a group of shady characters were stationed at the corner of Charlotte Street. And when the mother came out on the doorstep, with a heavy heart and red eyes, she had to suffer a hateful face-to-face encounter with the sniffers.

She saw them quite well, the sneering faces.

They were the same persons who had searched her, the same ones who had been her assiduous and refined executioners for one long month.

They were the ones who had killed her baby.

Ah! It is hard to believe. Is it necessary to name names? Is it necessary to give details?

Well then, the leader of the gang is named Melville. In his trade, he has the position of inspector. He is a kind-looking gentleman with an ingratiating way of speaking. And his collaborators are notorious throughout the French quarter of London. There is a huge devil of a corporal with broad shoulders, a bristly, reddish mustache and a boxer's fists. Then there is a slightly paunchy chap, with brown muttonchops, grizzled hair and the imperturbable face of a comfortable merchant. The two partners were a steadfast pair and, even though their cover was blown, went stubbornly snooping about. Then there's the hodge-podge of ponces and bootblacks who augment the incomes from their more or less avowed trades with the small benefits reserved for snitches. We know them.

Among nearly a dozen endeavors too long to list, Melville made one that was particularly edifying, and its terms deserve to be reported word for word.

On the afternoon of Monday, August 1, while Delbecque was at his workshop, the inspector managed to get into the house with Delbecque's female companion, and he addressed her using all the tricks of the trade, sometimes with promises, sometimes with threats.

"Look, you are suffering, your baby daughter is wasting away. Be reasonable, what the heck? Aren't you tired of this dead-end struggle? I want to get you out of this impasse. Listen to me. You need a rest, a peaceful life... this is all available to you. It only requires you to admit to me that Meunier has lived here, to show me his new hideout, and you will be guaranteed a peaceful existence. It will be guaranteed to you, to your six children, even to your husband! What more can I say?

"Don't lose your patience. No one will know. It will remain between us. If you don't want to listen to me, so much the worse! But your husband will not keep his job, you can be sure of that. We've been informed. And then your brats…

"Come on now, try to understand. It is in your interest. You are a courageous wife, a good mother. It will be a fine thing when your children cry from hunger. Hold on, here's what I propose to you: five hundred pounds. And that is just a start. Five hundred pounds right away!

"You refuse me, okay: I'll go. But think, think well—you have till tomorrow, so think it over: your husband without work, your children without bread…"

## Ta-ra-ra-boom-de-ay!

There are fine people who still have it in for the English, because they burnt Joan of Arc. If some of our fellow countrymen were implicated in the case, let's say a bishop, this wicked Frenchman would have been quite worthy of being English:

"All Englishmen are Cauchons[12]!"

The latest devotees of the virgin of Domrémy assert it with conviction. Obviously, they go too far. Still, by god, I prefer their fervent exaggeration to the endless "all rights" of the irritating anglophiles.

---

12 A wordplay on *cochons* (pigs) and the followers of Pierre Cauchon (1371-1445 CE), bishop of Beauvais and president of the court of Reims, who condemned Joan of Arc to the stake.

## English Holiday

At the time of the last elections, the majority of French newspapers lauded the exemplary spectacle that these elections offered in England. Even the adamant opponents of parliamentarianism themselves sweetened their pens to describe the steeplechases that run on the electoral racetracks of Great Britain.

And they call these fair elections!

In fact, a more degrading comedy has probably never been staged.

Throughout the city, you could see coaches everywhere, decorated with ribbons and driven by coachmen with multi-colored rosettes in their buttonholes. These festively decked-out holiday carts went in search of voters in their homes—one after another. And the voter went down and took his place in the cart or taxi, with the propagandists of a candidate seated to his right and to his left. It was free passage to the ballot box. The docile voter nearly disappeared, jostled between the two bulky partners who preached at him. Resigned, he let himself be driven to vote... and really no, nowhere else, would the poor sovereign people have to make such a sad face.

Here the aspiring members of parliament, who end up taking the voters for a ride[13], first give them a ride in a coach. It's the custom here. You have to agree: there are fewer prejudices here than in Loches, for example, where a candidate was disqualified for that very reason.

---

13 The original French here is "*mener leurs électeurs en bateau*", which literally means "taking their voters on a boat." But this is slang in French for lying to someone or giving them a cock-and-bull story. I figured that "taking their voters for a ride" kept the wordplay mostly intact.

It is fitting to emphasize that the candidate was named Wilson—another English name.

If all this doesn't seem very serious, it gets better.

The revolutionaries here, who come to London trusting in the traditional hospitality, fall into a trap...

The symptoms are convincing.

The "siren" entices the exiles with her promises of freedom and encourages them to let down their guard. They arrive openly. They are welcomed. Expulsion is unknown! Yes, but spying is constant. The refugees are followed, they are questioned about their addresses and their jobs. It's like revolutionaries are corralled on the island. They are kept under surveillance and available—there is an understanding with the continent.

Tomorrow, there might be a raid!

One has to expect the worst from people whose business sense is so developed that they must instinctively accept every profitable deal.

Institutional liberalism is only a word. One has the right to rest on Sunday, but not to work as one pleases. And so it is, in the nitty-gritty details, an endless optical illusion.

I admire the philosophy of these exiles, as they repeat:

"Since we are foreigners, we aren't concerned with what happens here. We won't compromise our shelter. We'll keep quiet."

This reasoning sounds false. If we had wanted to remain silent, we wouldn't be here. We left the cities where we liked living, because, first of all, we wanted to openly express our rebellion. We have not changed since. And we will continue to denounce the base acts of those countries where fate... and the police... drive us.

At the moment, we're in England, so let's speak of hypocrisy.

Isn't it affirmed that individual liberty is sacred, that the home is inviolable?

Let's take a little look.

Just a week ago, in the middle of the night, twenty individuals with revolvers in hand invaded a house on Campton Street. These men were not, as one might think, poor devils in need, but rather common criminals—the police. After climbing onto the roof and smashing windowpanes one by one, they tumbled through a window overlooking the stairs. The owner awoke with a start and leapt out of bed, shouting:

"Who goes there?"

No answer. The officers spread out on every floor of the house and broke through doors with their shoulders, terrorizing tenants who were surprised in their sleep. They used force to enter a sick woman's room. Nothing stopped them. The dwelling was quickly turned upside-down, from cellar to attic. The invaders searched, rummaged in the furniture, read correspondence they found. And when the gang leader finally deigned to explain:

"We thought that you were hiding someone," he said, "someone we're searching for. Good night! We had the wrong house."

The next morning, the people whose house had been so outrageously violated went to the judge. English judges, it is said, are impartiality in the flesh—they are asked to export it. At least the plaintiffs will be avenged.

"How could this happen, here among us?" the honest judge cries. "It is improper. It is shocking. The home must be respected. Justice will be done… What a shame that I can do nothing about it."

"How's that?"

"It isn't in my jurisdiction. Still you won't fail to get satisfaction. Contact the police."

"But they were the ones who did it."

"They are the ones concerned."

During the course of the day, an inspector of public safety did, indeed, present himself at Campton Street. He was provided with full powers and came to settle things—sacred things!

Since time is money, his speech is quite concise:

"Here are twenty-five francs, sir, you've been paid back.—Let's not speak of it anymore…"

And the newspapers were silent. No protest arose. The citizens of free Albion had their share of complicity.

The good faith of these islanders is now no longer open to debate. When they explain their principles in detail, they give the impression of dancing a jig.

It is the national virtue.

Ta-ra-ra-boom-de-ay! Ta-ra-ra-boom-de-ay!! They sing the popular refrain—and it doesn't mean a thing.

The old English reputation doesn't mean a thing anymore.

*Chapter 4*

# THE LONG TREK

### **Aimless**

"So, as they say, what is their aim?"

And the good-hearted questioner suppresses a shrug while noting that there are young men who defy the customs, the laws, the demands of the current society, but who don't affirm any program.

"What is their aspiration?"

If only these negators without creed had the excuse of fanaticism; but no, faith no longer wants to be blind. They discuss, they grope, they search. Pitiful tactic! These skirmishers in the social conflict, these flagless ones, have the aberration of not proclaiming that they possess the only formula for universal cure-alls. Even Mangin[14] had more spirit.

"And their interest, I ask you?"

Let's not talk about it. They don't crave commissions or posts or delegations of any sort. They are not candidates. What then? Let me laugh!

They have a fitting contempt for them, a contempt mixed with pity.

I have my share of this contempt.

We are those with quite strong feelings, though we scarcely catch a glimpse of future truths.

Nothing more ties us to the past, but the future is not yet clear.

And necessarily, we are badly understood like strangers; here, there, everywhere, we are strangers.

Why?

Because we do not want to recite new catechisms nor, in particular, to pretend to believe in the infallibility of doctrines.

We would need a cowardly complacency to show unreserved acceptance of a bunch of theory. We have no complacency at all. There was no Revelation: we keep our enthusiasm virgin for one Passion. Will it come?

Besides, even if the final end escapes us, we don't avoid our task. Our era is one of transition, and the free man has his part to play.

---

14 General Charles Mangin (1866-1925), raised in the Saint-Cyr military academy lik Zo d'Axa, embodied the prototype of the colonial officer, tireless, spirited, a man who dominates men and forced events. Convinced of the valor of the Senegalese troops with which he had fought, he was a partisan fro a black army in the service of France.

We hate authoritarian society, we prepare the experimentation of a libertarian society.

Though uncertain of what it might bring, we truly desire this endeavor—this change.

Rather than stagnating in this aging world where the air is oppressive, where the ruins fall as if to bury us, we hasten its final demolition.

In order to hasten the hour of rebirth.

## No Matter Where

I have said: strangers everywhere!

Yes, not much less in Paris than in this London where I've been vegetating for three months on an exile's vacation.

Here, for instance, you don't even get superficially acclimatized. You can't overcome the reserve of the natives or penetrate even minimally into the surrounding environment. You feel like you are concretely set apart. And the isolation lies heavy in the thick sadness of the fog.

It is useless to visit the international clubs; they are disappointing. The solidarity of certain revolutionary groups has the ostentation of charity; the distressing show goes on. And what's more, every aggressive suspicion slips in, pouring cold water on the spontaneity of the impulses. Accusations fly back and forth. Dispute and invective take precedence over discussion.

Mistrust reigns.

You have to go back to your room and find yourself alone there. But this little room that opens out on the courtyard, on the bottom floor of a seedy house, is nostalgic.

You can count the number of exiles who enjoy a comfortable home on your fingers. The others drag their steps, unconsciously drawn toward the neighborhoods of Whitechapel, over there, behind the Tower of London; They wander through the miserable alleys and throw themselves back onto the main arteries when the teeming crowd leaves the factories and warehouses, growing deep like a tide in which it would be good to drown.

As they pass through the big cities, the rich boulevards or city buildings no longer interest them. They even visit the museums only occasionally, since the technical works and conceptions of the past that can still move them are rare. Monuments possess only the beauty of their harmony, and when this superb whole is lacking, they rise like old rocks that a historical memory is not adequate to exalt.

Well then, it is still exciting to search for the salient traits of a race by making contact with the soul of the people. One goes into the lower city among the stalls of the small tradesmen, on the streets where the kids grow up running around barefoot, in the paths where here and there, tumbledown hovels, vast apartment blocks, popular projects that seem like giant beehives for beggars stand out.

The cells of these hives are narrow, the dividing walls of the hovels are thin, and they have no fireplaces. The life squeezed into hovels overflows into the muddy street, which is occasionally gifted with a ray of sunlight, with the commotion of an anthill.

In the open, in full light, a job is perpetually reborn; and pale women wash coarse linens and cook potatoes on braziers, stirred by the wind, for the meal that will be consumed there, sitting by the door on wobbly chairs. And these people know each other, shout back and forth, move, exist in a particular life, with characteristic manners, specific habits, original minds and customs whose brutal side evokes the primitive aspect of the species.

In London, I have always sensed hostility, even in the looks that set harshly as if to prohibit approach: Go on!

Each Englishman mysteriously symbolizes the country: these islanders seeming like so many unapproachable little islands in which the sap of the plants is not aroused by warm tones.

And it is monotonous, it is neutral, it is gray... And I've had enough!

Time to set off!

Oh! It is not that I have any illusions of getting a brotherly welcome elsewhere. The exile knows that every refuge is uncertain, he knows well that he will be looked upon with suspicion in Geneva as well as Brussels, in Spain as well as Italy... But in the end, when he is tired of staying in one place, it is clear that he has no need for a goal when he heads out on the road.

Time to set off, for any place whatsoever...

On a trek! Going, escaping melancholy. At first, every place has its charm: everything is beautiful, at least for an hour.

Wisdom lies in not staying.

Passing through, gathering impressions, enjoying the new sensations and flavors of the lands. And then taking to the road again, always! Perhaps toward some unreachable homeland. Vagabond, pilgrim, tramp, in exploration, in conquest; insatiable as Don Juan, with a higher love: the dress one wants to rip off is a mist on the horizon.

The deep, green Thames carries so many adventurous desires over its waters.

After Westminster, after the tower, after the port, at Blackwall, it widens. Great ships glide toward the sea and their whistles are calls that one cannot hear without flinching…

And at Blackwell one morning, I took the ferry to Holland without much forethought. With a few more shillings in my wallet, I would have embarked to visit Sweden or to see Calcutta.

## Traveling Musicians

The passage from London to Rotterdam lasts a day and a night. The cost is not excessive: fifteen francs in third class. And the lowest class for a short sea voyage is not appreciably worse than first class. It's enjoyable to stay on the deck and watch the picturesque coasts that slip by, then to think, even contemplating the battle of the waves and the sky off the coast sinking into the water.

For this show in infinity, every place is pretty much the same, from stem to stern.

Besides, third class is required when all one has is a few Louis. This is the case with me, and my baggage is light and the velvet of my clothes is rustic.

In third class, one meets few people who are traveling for pleasure. There are only poor people who are returning to their native countries, and workers who hope to find work far from their city.

Not one tourist.

## The Long Trek

Even the most modest of them want to have their ease and comfort. They prefer to wait until their piggybanks fill up so that they can at least travel in second class; they embark with full satchels, a round trip ticket and the various coupons for the agreed-upon hotels. The invaluable advantage of third class is not to have to mix with them.

The insipid chatter of the Perichons[15] is never more painful than on the majesty of the open sea.

It's like a pursuit.

And the childish conversations of the between-deck passengers, of the penniless folks who don't put on a pose and let out their untarnished feelings, are better. No more irritating flow and affected recitals of triumphant clichés: they talk of hopes and worries. And depending on the time and the hour, colorful words gush out.

When it happens in third class that chance sometimes arranges the best companionship, it's a stroke of good fortune. I went down the Thames in the friendly company of some hard-working troubadours who paid their way by playing the waltzes of their country from time to time.

Tanned faces on agile Bohemian bodies and frenzied violins. They were returning from a trip around the Scottish countryside.

They were emigrating to escape the winter.

Some of them spoke French and told me about their nomadic life. It was pleasant and appealingly reckless. They traveled along their road—sun, open air and music.

I was with them too short a time.

---

15 An old French aristocratic family.

Settled at the boat's bow, camped on the luggage, while the violins rested in their linen cases, our careless eyes followed the sure movements of the tugboats and the caprices of the sailboats.

Fewer gloomy factories bordered the river; there were lakes of red earth where sheep grazed on sparse grass. The Thames widened again. It was Greenwich, and at dusk, we felt the lapping of the waves.

It was the sea.

I didn't recognize the strange melodies with which my companions greeted it, but their instruments and their voices harmonized with the sound of the waves in a rocking rhythm.

In the night, the salty breeze was our appetizer. We were hungry and someone cut long pieces of ham as we passed around a comradely flask of whiskey…

We reached Rotterdam the next day and went down into a portside inn. And while a concert was improvised, I went to look at the old houses with their uneven roofs, sitting neatly on the canals of this rather crude Venice.

The musicians told me that they were staying for two weeks. That was more than I could do: best wishes, good-by! hand clasps…

A bit further, at its mouth, the Rhine brought me the enduring reflection of its old castles. The same imperious desire that caused me to go down one river urged me to go up the other. The Thames, the Rhine! Is it not like the extension of a great tempting road?

## The Barge

In the noisy cabarets of the seaside cities, where mechanics and seamen knock them back between voyages, you meet the kind sailors who, for a few drinks, offer you the means for traveling.

Most of the merchant ships accept a nonpaying passenger, if needs be, either to make use of him on board or because a crewmember presents him as an old friend. That was how an easy-going bargeman presented me to the captain of a barge heading for Mannheim.

It cost me three glasses of Dutch gin.

The barge sailed up every navigable part of the Rhine in twelve days, lightening its load of sugar and aniline[16] at various stops. Going slowly forward against the current, stopping along the way in the cities, Köln, Bonn, Ober Lahntein or Mainz, you get an impression of the country very much at your leisure.

Life on board was simple. I had brought some frugal provisions, Dutch cigars among them, and spent a long time leaning on piles of rope from where I witnessed the uninterrupted procession as I smoked.

Dortrecht, gracious in the calmness of its wooded banks. And the tranquility of the plains: Tiel. Lobit, the German border which is indicated merely by a peaceful, little customs-house. Emmerich with the gothic belltowers. Duesburg with the Krupp factory, the manufacturing plants; a somber and harsh mining town so close and yet so far from the delightful Dutch shores: there is no more life, just the struggle for it. We come into Germany. The access to small villages is aggressively protected by slopes adorned with cannons. You notice a nation that polishes weapons.

---

16 A chemical used in making dyes and pharmaceuticals.

It is—with the other preparations—like a bronze rhyme.

Dusseldorf, then quickly Köln. The two towers of the cathedral stand out so unpleasantly adjoined that, despite the working of the finely chiseled stone, they form a single pile of obsessive weight. An afternoon passed wandering randomly through the city. In the museum, Albrecht Dürer and Caron the Elder, delicate and naïve, irreparably damage the Rubens exhibition. Commercial activity, the traffic of the port zone. And at dusk, we leave for Bonn, the legendary university where romantic students still sport proud scars.

Then Koblenz and the Ehrenbreitstein fortress on the craggy rock.

The most picturesque parts of the river flow between there and Mainz: Ober Lahntein. Steep cliffs with broken-down castles, those of St-Goar, the Mouse opposite the Cat, with trees growing out of the large cracks in the turrets.

The vineyards among the rocks.

Proud villages on hills that wreathe the feudal dwelling at the end of a twisted path. The color is smoke-gray, sometimes with the clear and warm tone of Roman ruins. The red, fern-covered fields, the white graveyard, the pointed roofs of the village, the tiny, proud old church. Everything Medieval gothic; an audacious harmony that fit the rugged nature, amidst the lofty rustling of poplars.

And the Rhine grazes the rocks more quickly.

At Mainz, there are groups of soldiers on fatigue duty walking about.

The sound of swords fills the streets.

The image of a superb nature that opened on this side of the forts of Koblenz dies away on the flat banks near Mainz, the soldiers' city.

And the distinctive sign would go unsaid:

An intensity of poetry framed by militarism.

## From Cities to Country Villages

On the busy docks of Mannheim, where the Rhine and the Neckar converge, I left the hospitable barge, which had completed its itinerary and was loading a cargo of lumber to take back on the return trip.

As easy and inexpensive as it is to travel the large rivers, when you travel by land with little money, you run into many difficulties every step of the way. The problems are complicated if you aren't very familiar with the language of the place: I took the wrong road twice on my way to Heidelberg.

But you are well repaid for your effort when you arrive in the ancient and solemn capital of the Lower Palatinate.

All the roads climb up, losing themselves in the green darkness of the mountain.

And the incomparable castle, fantastic apparition, with a well, tunnels, huge rooms, kitchens in whose fire pits whole bulls were cooked, cellars where enormous casks—one with a capacity of three hundred thousand liters—have been filled time and again by the peasants' tithes…

And what remains of the main towers, stone upon stone, imposing blocks, dilapidated walls, onto which you hoist yourself to better observe the surrounding landscape, the intriguing abyss of the valley below.

The ancient trees shake the tangle of their colorful plumes, the highest of which ripple so nearby that they caress the ruins at your feet. And that shimmering tumult of green is as seductive as a fluffy bed with a hint of velvet.

It looks like something soft that you could throw yourself into.

Besides, wouldn't the wind that blows so strongly and howls through the threatening cracks sweep you away if you didn't hang on tight?

Little shivers run through your legs, breaking the giddy fascination, and you head back down through the ruggedness of grinding wheels.

And for a long time after leaving the castle, on the paths through the pines, you continue to see the magical vision of the landscape immersed in the shrubby meanderings of the Neckar.

It's the background of promised lands.

Strangely, you might try to mark out your path from to villages, and never grow tired—toward villages and cities.

Onward! Let's go and look further.

Triberg, the Black Forest where I lived for almost a week, staying in the low house of a wood-cutter who was ugly as a gnome.

The kirsch in that shed was good.

I went out in the early morning to take in the wild scents of the fierce forest air—a forest so thick that the midday sun was barely able to brighten its foliage. And what a startling contrast when suddenly tawny boulders rose up, desperate, which only a few thin shrubs climb, as if to attack.

Nature speaks.

I gained a better understanding of the human sense of torrents from the cascades that roared over large polished rocks. I enjoyed the fieriness of reddish waters that persevered all the more against the obstacle of great, uprooted trees...

What a shame not to be able to adventure in this countryside longer, even for weeks or months! What a pain not to be able to continue on foot, knapsack on my back, through that beautiful landscape!

The last coins jingled in my pocket.

At the next city through which the train passed, I was barely able to pay for a ticket to Milan. I counted on getting provisions through some Italian friends.

I confess that I took the iron path.

## Young Girls

In Milan, this afternoon, young girls were on trial.

And it wasn't the sad trial of the surprised child on a bench with a harsh judge, of course *in absentia*.

I watched the hearing as it unfolded.

It concerned an anarchist demonstration where, along with the resolute men and bold women, they arrested two young girls—aged fourteen and fifteen.

The brunette, Maria, had a strange charm, with her determined gait, like a headstrong lad, those short curls and fiery black eyes. She had a way of looking over the gentlemen of the court that was a kind of silent, intangible insolence—it was better than throwing a boot.

And when she spoke, it was not the florid speech that rouses a smile; her short phrases meant something and were heightened by sure gestures.

"How can you talk to each other about making anarchy?" the judge grumbled, "You don't know what it is."

"So then, have you studied anarchy better? Then it exists. Will you teach me about it?"

No, little one, they have nothing to teach you! Rebellion is instinctive. And far too often, theory is childish. You know everything if you feel the stain of living a stupid life.

Ernesta Quartiroli, a year younger, has no less distinctive features. Her budding beauty is serious—enigmatic. She could be a proud statue of the meaningful future: who knows?

Her silence is haughty. It seems that the problem is not hers. A yes, a no, a shrug and that's all.

But Maria Roda, the brunette, with her defiant attitude, does not allow the parade of prosecution witnesses to continue its tiresome procession uninterrupted. Her retorts mark out the breaks. She stops the shameful snitches and the professional squealers in their tracks.

She has a retort for everyone, a retort that hits the mark.

A Public Security agent recites the lesson he learned against her: "Miss Roda incited demonstrators to let fly against the police, she struggled like one possessed, heckled everybody, even insulted a corporal!…"

"How do you respond?" the judge asked.

"I feel sorry for this guard. I feel sorry for him because he barely earns enough to feed himself, because he is a poor devil; but it disturbs me to see him attacking other poor devils: his brothers… Let him think about that."

And with a pardoning gesture toward the miserable fellow who had just accused her, she may have cast the first revealing light into that dark mind.

## The Long Trek

At the age when others have barely left their dolls behind, at the age when daughters of the bourgeoisie begin their love-games with a young cousin or an old family friend, these girls showed themselves to be the comrade-sisters.

Prison is imposed. The men of the court were generous. Ernesta and Maria would get three months in jail—and the youngsters would have to pay a fine to these gentlemen.

Three hundred francs demanded of the poor young girls!...

It's cynical, but that's how it is... Besides, as long as there's hair under the judge's wig, won't there be lovelocks?[17]

A moment before the court recessed to cook up the grounds for the condemnation, the man in red asked Maria:

"Do you have anything to add?"

"Nothing! Since it would all be useless!"

And it was the last word, not very cheerful, but cutting.

It is said again and again that Milan is a little Paris. Milanese judges show this on at least one point: they are just as completely repulsive as their Parisian colleagues.

But isn't the magistrature the same everywhere? And could it be any other way?

Perhaps this is why the memory of the homeland remains with you as you pass through every country. It comes back up as a nausea when you see the vileness of judges.

---

17 The French word, *rouflaquette*, literally means sideburns, a style considered attractive to women at the time, but the word is also slang for pimps and other men who made their money by using and bullying women.

## Know the Country!

The plunderers of villas generally operate at night. Italian police chiefs, most of whom started out as independent burglars before they started working in the service of the moustached king, have maintained their original aversion to daytime occupations.

Three in the morning is judged to be an especially propitious time for invading other people's homes and taking possession of the chosen objects. These fellows aren't just looking for individuals to accuse; they are also searching for foreign tobacco, cigarette cases, rings and photographs of young women…

The Piedmontese police chief is an eclectic thief.

In one of the dialects that make up the Italian language, they call this nocturnal bird Signor Delegato.[18]

From this, you can readily understand that he is, effectively, a representative—the representative of official banditry.

Almost everyone is aware of this. It is well-known that, with trains and the Savoy monarchy, Calabrian customs have spread quickly throughout the peninsula. Every day, cheerfully cleaned-out tourists return through the Modane, bringing at least one string of edifying anecdotes. But usually they had a brush specifically with innkeepers, guides and antique sellers. Those who tell stories about the cops were usually not themselves the victims. As for me, I can speak first-hand. And I didn't just see, I also felt—I felt the handcuffs.

There were eight of them on that night last week, when they came to disturb my virtuous sleep lulled by pleasant

---

18 Mr. Representative.

dreams. I dreamed of leaving Turin—the monotonous city, for Spain, for Barcelona. There were eight of them little trilby hats and poet's neckties. With their revolvers in hand. They broke down the doors, and dimmed the lights. They looted my luggage and we're on our way to the police station.

Surely they don't want to make me go on foot? The leader of the small-hats had already implied as much: "It's not too far and at this hour we won't find a carriage on the street."

I had to explain to him that in that case, his men would have to carry me—and by force. It really was necessary to find carriages; they found one. That was to be a disappointment for the police chief. He made an ugly face when he had to give up the idea of pocketing the expenses of the trip.

But could I let myself be seen in such company? Those people reeked of the police station from miles away. And if we had crossed paths with some night owl, in order to avoid the worst confusion and at least justify myself in the eyes of the passerby, I would have shouted: "I'm not a cop, I'm the criminal!"

I soon learned my crime. At the police station, there was a semblance of an inquiry. And I learned everything from an inspector who tried to interrogate me:

"You are the editor of *L'Endehors*!"

That's it, all of it. Now this is qualification enough, pretty much everywhere in Europe, for getting hauled off to prison.

That's how it is. Governments issue the order. The prosecutor's office waits in ambush behind the traps of exceptional laws, servile jurors willing condemn, and there at the borders, authority keeps watch to arrange some nasty trick.

The police inspector also let me know that, furthermore, if it were possible, my situation would get worse. In fact, the day before, I had written and sent an article by certified mail about a very recent trial held in Milan. The violators of the cubbyhole had already gone through it. Even before the article was published, it was condemned. I deserved a lesson.

When pimps on a deserted street corner jump a passing latecomer, ten against one, they don't let anyone run up to intervene. A single word triggers the pack of hounds. In the same way, civilized countries don't allow a foreigner to concern himself with their affairs—cruelly dirty. They generally admit it, shamelessly:

"We will grant you hospitality, but you have to keep your mouth shut."

Shut up! Remaining passive as atrocities are committed right before our eyes, as masters torture slaves, as judges condemn innocent people; in a word, disarming ourselves as this society clamps down—never! We would no longer be ourselves And we have the pride to want to keep our pen ready.

One after another, the governments can make us compare their prisons. We are the incorrigibles who any suppression spurs on. As soon as we get out of prison, we are ready to become repeat offenders. Chased out of here, we will go there. The world is big.

In my case, for the time I will no longer be carrying my walking stick around Italy.

After half a week in the Turin jail, I was informed that I'd been expelled from the kingdom. They prevented me from going to Genoa, where I had hoped to catch a boat to Spain. But they gave me the choice between Modane,

## The Long Trek

Chiasso and Cormons. The French border didn't seem advisable to me. Switzerland is an insipid country if you are not an Englishman with a good private income, Austria was the only one left. Cormons is not far from Trieste. And Trieste was the sea with its free horizon.

The journey was not amusing.

Two *carabinieri* were waiting for me at the office of the clerk of the court. They clamped my wrists tightly in an ingenious device that was then bolted to padlock. Then the classic paddy wagon brought us to the station. Milan was the first stop. I was taken down to the city hotel where the boys in uniform scrupulously locked the door. Just two days later, we returned to our journey, this time as far as Verona, where there was a new stopover in a prison that wasn't much filthier than the last one. Finally, on the fifth, freed from the repugnant escort, let out of the improved carriage, I crossed the border—my hands made blue by the irons.

A bit of detail wouldn't be out of place. It is good to inform our friends in Paris. It is good for them to recognize the special treatment you enjoy in Mignon.

This country where pickpocket functionaries flourish is a poorly cleared land where every kind of propaganda is possible—the brilliance would not be harmful.

Recently cleansed of religious superstition, the people are being driven in a herd toward the patriotic delusion. Few people think.

The leaders jealously maintain this state of moral sluggishness. And this is the reason for the dread inspired by anyone who wants to throw a thought into the minds of the poor.

They tell themselves that we might actually open the eyes of some unaware dispossessed person. They shudder at the idea of contagion…

And the quarantines are hard…

The fact is that the virus of hatred and revolt can no longer be eliminated—once you have it there in your blood.

## After Expulsion

I ask myself if you used governmental suspicions and took advantage of successive expulsions—propellant forces that carry you across countries, couldn't you manage with a bit of good will to go around the world?

You could try.

Kicked out of Italy, I still avoided facilitating the continuation of my travels through the artless means of the Austrian police.

In Trieste, I took care not to be seen in full daylight with the comrades I met there by chance. They were very brave young men who published the eighth issue of a small socialist broadsheet, the first seven of which had suffered the sad fate of being seized.

In the evening, we met in a pub in Burgstrasse, and it was no run-of-the-mill pleasure for me to find the same rebellious tendencies, hundreds of miles from Paris, and to feel identical instincts and enthusiasms vibrating. We talked late into the night about the spreading movement, about all the scattered efforts that are multiplying and growing like so many eruptions converging toward the ideal of freedom.

And I spent the days wandering on the docks where slender steamships landed upon their return from unknown shores.

## The Long Trek

Amid the cries and the endless merry-go-round of the porters, heavy bales of cotton, crates of oranges and loaves of date bread in sacks woven from heavy grass fibers were unloaded. There were the mysteriously packed goatskins, white rice from India, bananas and aromatic wood from the islands. In addition the things that novice seamen cheerfully bring back from their first voyages: the monkey gamboling on a leash, the large, multicolored birds. And the trade of the bazaar merchants who sold gazelle horns, Turkish pipes, Algerian guns and tawny jungle plunder.

There you saw the entire orient...

You need to know some of these harbors of the Mediterranean basin, to understand how much this enchanting evocation of the Levant and the daily view of departing steamships rouses your desire to head out to sea in your turn.

Naples or Algiers, more seductive, more colorful, may not evoke this desire for exotic flight so much.

Living there is much too sweet.

Trieste, on the contrary, shaken by the wind, the kisses of the Adriatic Gulf, gives the sirens' song a greater intensity; you desire to escape drab Europe and sail toward the distance of a sun-drenched dream.

After visiting Italy—I had waited for the amnesty of 1889 in Rome and Florence—I planned to complete a vision of antiquity in Greece.

For this reason, I thought about Athens for years.

The opportunity presented itself to me; my curiosity didn't waver for long.

On the decks and piers there was always an impatient crowd of Turks, Montenegrins, Egyptians in fezzes and

Palikares[19] in their pleated skirts. A colorful population, coming and going, getting lost in the search for ships setting sail. A bizarre, gesticulating world, bumping into each other and embracing each other in the snarl of baggage and the confusion of farewells.

To reach the ships, boatmen's voices offered the promise of longboats: "Monsieur! Signore! Mein Herr! Corfu, Patras, Epirus?"

All right then! and I jumped on a small boat.

## The Useful Knife

There were fifteen Italians on board the "Pandora" who were going to the mines of Laurium. Some of them had not yet done their military service, and so, to avoid endless and notoriously difficult paperwork in Venice, they had to come to Trieste to embark.

We were soon acquainted.

The Austrian Lloyd Company's ship was supposed to take us as far as Patras on the eastern tip of Peloponnesus. From there the emigrants were supposed to continue the journey like me, on the train that travels the entire width of the peninsula.

But a significant annoyance delayed our arrival: with cholera as a pretext, we spent five days under surveillance in the quarantine station in Corfu.

The company had asked us for five guilders each in addition to the price of the voyage: a guilder per person per day

---

19 A name given to Greek independence fighters.

for the period of the quarantine. – After all, it was paid! We had organize ourselves in such a way as to not live too badly together – you no longer considered the little inconveniences.

The ship cast off under a good wind.

We tacked, rarely losing sight of the coast.

The shoreline was aglow with light. The warm lips of the bays smiled with their white houses.

Dalmatia. The terraces of old Ragusa. Centinje camped wildly on the Montenegrin cliffs.

On the third day at dawn, we cast anchor in the deep waters of Brindisi.

The ship was close to the large dock, so that a simple gangplank was enough to go down onto the land. In the high part of the city, the square tower of a cathedral formed a somber mass, and in the pale light of the morning I saw this grim picture up nearby:

Four by four, a line of jailbirds with dirty brown jackets and numbered red caps walked along the shore, dragging the ball and chain. In front of them, behind them, to their right, and to their left, jailers were on the watch with rifles ready.

A sad procession! It was the last image that Italy left me...

And I thought about human justice, the justice that would have stuck me in prison if I had set foot on land: for transgression of an expulsion order! Justice thirty feet away!

On the boat I was a free man; it I had tread on Italian soil, I would have become a repeat offender.

We moved away.

Soon we saw the Albanian coast, vast solitude of rocky wilderness, bleak space along the broken line of the surf.

In Corfu, many ships seemed to be doing penance and were now and then brought to a stop. And in the gulf, the yachts used by the health inspection made you sad. Everwhere, the yellow flags at half mast.

The quarantine began badly.

They claimed that the money we paid didn't give us the right to food for the five days. It was just a fee for the place we occupied.

They didn't provide us with sleeping cots or even blankets, or any shelter except the corridors near the engine room and kitchens where sometimes the fine aroma of roasting meat prevailed.

Despite this valuable benefit, a guilder a day for our "storage" was real rip-off. And even less bearable since most of us, convinced that we needed food, had spent our money royally.

So the news did not pass without causing a certain commotion that I kept alive, you can believe me. Would you passively suffer the dirty tricks of the Company?

I was delegated to go to the Captain.

I demanded that the amount paid be given back to us; we would put up with quarantine on land, at the quarantine station on the small island nearby where bunkers had been built on the ruins of a fortress. Our little tribe would know how to arrange a way to eat.

The captain flatly refused.

There was just one way left to us – we rowdily went to install ourselves in first class.

It was an rout.

The Italians, with their hobnail boots and huge backpacks, their resolute looks and huge beards, seemed more like hosts than suspects.

They made their demand in song: bread.

Some passengers thought that there was a rebellion on board and fled to the cabins.

The captain rushed in, this time with good words. We would be fed, there had been a mistake, we had a right to the same rations as the sailors...

Since we weren't hard to please, we shouted: "Long live the commander!"

But as we returned to our quarters, the emigrants became sarcastic and ironically prolonged their cheer.

Curious sorts, these Piedmontese, insolently deferential, with reckless audacity, they wander around the world as hirelings – captains of labor.

There are thousands of them. The country had no more use for their arms; living at home became impossible: no jobs! They leave to go in search of hazardous work.

They're the ones who crowd helter-skelter onto ships heading for South America; they'll be bold pioneers. They're the ones who populate work-sites of the railroad line advancing across the African plains. They're also the ones we find, at certain times of year, for the hardest jobs in the fields in Belgium, Germany, France.

Sedentary workers don't like these adventurers without unions or dues.

They're bringing wage rates down!

But who are the culprits? The masters, the bosses, as always! They abuse a condition imposed on the hungry: accepting a paltry wage or dying of starvation.

The instinct for self-preservation speaks louder than any feeling of solidarity; it's natural – and so they sign on to work.

The bullying begins: filthy Italians! Macaronis! And since they can't be beaten with impunity, they are reproached for using the knife.

This knife is useful.

From the moment you subject yourself to bourgeois exploitation, from the moment you start working, it is necessary to submit to the current laws of supply and demand.

The wage rate can't be imposed.

You still have to live.

It is no more degrading to rent oneself out for three francs than for six.

I prefer shirkers, recalcitrants, whoever they may be, all those who do nothing at all to run this machine, into which I will always throw a monkey wrench with pleasure.

But since in this society, the majority is made up of the resigned, and since wage rates are all that is being discussed, the Piedmontese wanderers have the right to deal in their way.

There is even an extreme pride in defending that right with blade in hand.

During the period of quarantine, the character of the emigrants revealed itself in many confessions – and this was an excellent study for me.

I appreciated the wild sense of their individualism.

It is the seed of rebellion.

We agreed.

The day before we parted, when I left for Patras, we had a party, a nourishing feast of polenta.

The Long Trek

## **Night Shelter**

In a light mist, iridescent under the sun, Patras appeared at the foot of the mountain, across from Missolonghi.

On the small square near the harbor, not far from the markets, the eagerness of a Sunday: European finery in garish colors and anachronistic styles. Church is getting out. The pretty faces of women, lost beneath the frameworks of their hats; old Greeks in national costumes: the short pleated petticoat, like a dancer—a multicolor, shimmering crowd that goes around like a carousel on the little square with three dusty palm trees.

On the terrace of a Moorish-style café, where anisette and 'mastic'[20] are served on low tables amidst saucers of olives, I have already devoutly given myself over to my first hookah.

The blond tobacco is slowly burning in the red earthen bowl, under the scented coal, while in the carafe with its copper framework the water hums in whimsical gurglings; the hookah stands like a priest and the long pipe stem with the triangular mouthpiece of opaque amber uncoils like the rings of some sacred serpent…

It's something else compared to a pipe.

And I mean that from the decorative point of view, there is an similar difference between the inhabitants of this country and those of ours. These Greeks have the marks of their origins. The lowest turkey driver has the innate distinction that our fine gentlemen seek in vain; with the delicacy of his features the peasant preserves this aristocratic trait imperiously expressing the glorious line of ancestors.

---

20 A natural gum made from the resin of the mastic tree.

This pride in their bearing, these casual manners, explain the carelessness that one notices in daily tasks; commerce doesn't rouse passion, agriculture is unconventional; I saw lettuce and rosebushes, potatoes and lilies mixed haphazardly in barbaric rows in the fields.

The train I took to Athens, one clear, sunny morning, stopped in all the stations along the golden route.

Constantly getting on and off, renewing themselves, the peasants snacked on dark bread and goat cheese to pass the time on the short journey; priests, long-haired beggars who filled pockets and saddle-bags on the trip to the nearest village and down-and-out soldiers who sang monotonous chants in nasal voices…

The tourists in the sleeping cars can't imagine how much an extended journey in a common local train shows you a population and allows you, in a way, to make contact with it.

The Klepht[21] goes into the city to get his supply of gunpowder. He seems to want to isolate himself in one corner of the compartment, with his pistol stocks slicing commas into his leather belt.

He has the burnoose of the Kabyles and also their typical audacity as well.

Parallels between the Greeks and Arabs[22] multiply.

The free mountaineer, shepherd, hunter, perhaps even collector of indirect taxes from strolling fat cats, he has the quiet majesty of a qadi[23] after the raid.

---

21 A member of the Greek armed bands in the struggle for independence against the Turkish empire.

22 Zo d'Axa was not aware that the Kabyles were Berbers, not Arabs.

23 A Moslem judge.

Here in the arid lowlands lies Megara, where the houses that are huts of red clay; you could call it a Saharan oasis under the burnt trees.

The scenery changes.

You go past a hill and there's Athens: dominating the style-less buildings of a provincial town, carved out geometrically to fit the lines of the streets, the cliff of the Acropolis, the pedestal of the Parthenon.

The Parthenon stands out in the flawlessness of its serene columns and the Acropolis seems like the last bastion of a superb past, contemptuous of the modern effort that gnaws at its foundations.

It is not that I exalt the relics of a world that has disappeared; but I tell myself: "Our world will leave nothing but rubbish!"

I don't at all feel the emotional respect of learned archeologists before ancient stones. At the stadium I had some reminiscence; the Illissus makes me think not so much of the Argonauts as of a high school, of tasks assigned as punishment, of student supervisors. High school! the first prison, academic procrustean bed, training for the barracks, a small society so foul that Society sprouts up there.

Besides, how can you isolate yourself, make the past come alive again, imagine warriors and chariots in these arenas… beside a tramline? How can you dream of paganism in these temples with rising out of excavations, and where Orthodox candles have as their vestals, sacred Virgins piously daubed with paint?

I didn't accompany the Englishmen who, equipped with a Baedeker, went to swoon over the sight of shapeless blocks, solely because this rubbish is listed in their guides. They don't allow themselves to miss a single bit of this rubbish, not one mutilated fragment, while their excited hands run across the bathhouse mosaics:

"Socrates passed by here!"

I rarely visit clinical museums: venerable pieces of statues, an arm of Venus, Apollo's leg, a labeled bust—the whole of surgical Greece!

As long as there are still works which impose their harmonious substance on my senses, primitive works, triumphant in the beauty of synthesis, the scurrying about of amateurs snooping about in that pile of famous rubble seems grotesque to me. Amphora handles, chips off bricks, pathetic fragments under glass… I look more thoughtfully at the rock that rolls in its endless wandering through the stream.

I arrived in Athens destitute.

I hoped to find a registered letter in the mail. Nothing. The wait lasted several days.

At the doors of restaurants, I sadly contemplated the suckling piglets that roasted in the most amusing poses and made due with meager portions in suburban greasy spoons.

Have I come to know the black broth[24]?

In any case, I remembered the philosophers who in the past slept in temple courtyards. One evening I reached the Parthenon and didn't come down until morning.

For the good reputation of this shelter without customers, I will say that, by way of morning soup, you enjoy a unique

---

24 A reference to an ancient Greek dish, made with simple ingredients, such as pork, blood and salt, with a semi-liquid consistency.

delicacy there: the awakening of the fair, trembling countryside at the feet of Hymettus.

## **The Dogs of Galatta**

I can't imagine any man traveling through Greece without going on into Turkey. It is always unpleasant to linger too long in one place or to turn back on one's steps, but here it would be more like suffering the mirages of Tantalus.

Greece only partially lifts a delicate veil on the Orient; you want to tear the curtain down.

And it's so easy: three times a week, a ferry leaves Piraeus heading for Constantinople – it takes thirty-six hours and costs twenty-five drachmas.

As soon as I had the twenty-five drachmas, I arranged the thirty-six hours.

At the mouth of the Bosforus, the immense capital extends into Europe and Asia. Constantinople is formed from three cities: Üsküdar on the Asian coast; Galata and Pera on the European coast with modern palaces; and the original city, Istanbul.

Istanbul! the boat glides over the calm sea that caressingly waters the gardens of sultans. It is Seraglio Point. The cacti and sycamores move gently like large fans, and in this feminine form of mysterious sensuality, minarets jut up like male calls.

We go around Seraglio Point, a pilot-boat acts as a guide among the steamships, sailboats and a certain number of caiques. The machine's uninterrupted whistle stresses its hectic signals, and the ship finally stops in front of the bridge that unites Istanbul and Galata, a drawbridge over the Golden Horn.

Galata is the lively old city, with shipping offices, inns for poor passengers, seamen's cabarets, muddy streets with large puddles that you have to jump.

It is the neighborhood of the slaughterhouses where the throat is slit according to the Muslim ritual: with the imam and the butcher. The officiant carries out an imitation with a gesture of his harmless sword. The assistants use ropes to drag the bull to the ground, holding its head backwards. The ready blade of the knife strikes the artery in the throat, the blood spurts, and even before the animal is dead, its flayed and cut into pieces. Another comes in, staggering, pulled and pushed by men with leather aprons blotched with red. The beast falters, and as it thrashes about with its throat cut, it gets flayed. The imam repeats his gesture: here are the imam and the butcher.

Galata is the brutal neighborhood where the stray dogs are the skinniest.

Almost every crossroad has its customary dog-pack that never makes any incursions into the neighboring streets.

But at night you hear extended barking from the outskirts, at the borders of Fera, the rich neighborhood on the hill. Could it be the undernourished dogs of Galata howling at other dogs who get an abundance of scraps at the doorsteps of luxurious houses?

On Friday morning, after being rather bored with the banality of Fera's shops, I found myself near the sultan's palace.

Midday was sounding, it was time for the *salaam*. The leader of the faithful was going to the mosque, allowing you to glimpse him behind a flank of his soldiers.

## The Long Trek

The palace is just a hundred meters from the Ahmediye mosque. On the turret, on top of the minaret, a muezzin made the call to prayer with arms raised.

Abdul-Hamid was seen in his half-covered carriage. The sultan is dressed in a black frock coat, without decorations, without insignia, with a fez on his head, with a deliberate simplicity that contrasts with the pashas in their decorated costumes that form a glittering procession of brocade and gold.

Three loud, long shouts greet His Omnipotence.

But Abdul-Hamid has already left his carriage and is climbing up the three steps of the mosque.

When the devotions have finished, the sultan reappears. Now he himself holds the reins of the two white horses that champ at the bit as they dash at a great trot toward the palace. The crowd of orderly officers, obese pashas, gasps for breath from the weight of the swords, in the flash of ironware. All the blazing uniforms mix, jostle and obsequiously move away from each other in the train of the gentleman in the frock coat, it seems to be a farce about a plebeian emperor.

Would you have any more Ottoman sensation in your peregrinations through Istanbul?

A boat goes up the Golden Horn as far as the fresh waters of Eyub, the village of the dead: White stones and cypresses along the streets where passers-by are rare and tombs embedded between the houses, in such a way that one might think a ghoulish market town had been built on a large graveyard. From Eyub, it is necessary to cross the whole of Istanbul to reach St. Sophia and the Bazaar. First, a sordid ghetto of tumbledown shacks, a sort of leper colony, where the Turk has penned in the Jews. From furrowed paths, one goes up stairways. Around the mosques, the air is purified; below, there's the clandestine life, here there is the intimate secret of locked, impenetrable houses: you imagine, behind the latticed windows, well-guarded pleasures of the harem.

Not one woman's face throughout the city, the combined muslins of the yachmak reveal only large, faraway eyes – and it is a refinement to have hidden lips.

There is more to desecrate.

Is modesty anything other than subtle depravity?

In the open, in the squares, vegetable and poultry vendors; the broad umbrellas of coarse cloth that shelter the tall seats where vendors and porters come to get a shave; the tripe-butcher's shop that trades mainly in boiled sheeps' heads; the gourmet tables of the dairyman: bowls of milk with almonds, honey and Turkish delight.

All the men where the red fez with the black tassle whether their costume is European or Turkish, not a hat.

In front of the mosques, whose domes rise up punctuated by minarets, in Schah-Sadeh, *Süleymaniye*, on the threshold of St. Sophia, at the fountain where the pigeons regularly descend, the Believers take off their shoes for the purifying ablution.

In the great bazaar, a maze of galleries, is a city covered with thousands of passageways, almost like boulevards, and often the dark bottleneck of dead ends, and everywhere, without interruption, boxes, counters, shops crowded with trained working people: a kind of gigantic temple of Commerce: or rather isn't it like a giant temple of Commerce?

Everything is for sale there: from the richest fabrics of Armenia and Baghdad, diamonds from Capetown, perfumes and pure essences in jeweled flasks, to vulgar trinkets and Turkish items from the Parisian bazaar.

At the center, weapons of Damascus steel, daggers inlaid with gold, long rifles with butts decorated with precious stones, and small sabers for children at 0.95. Outside the bazaar, in the adjacent streets, the intrusive stands, the stalls of second-hand dealers, niches of a sort, one inside or on top of the other, like a game of patience.

And still, in the promiscuity of the little shops, the camp of wooden shacks where so many families, on which it endlessly lives, are lodged, at the mercy of a cigarette, thrown perhaps without being extinguished, every little shack doomed to go up in flames.

One night, the watchman on patrol, who taps the pavement with his heavy cane to mark the hour, starts striking very rapidly and shouting; in his wake, a clamor arose on the avenue, repeated and sent back in echoes. There's a fire in Istanbul. Fire! Fire!

A screaming crowd rushes from all sides; it rushes from Galata, on the run, toward the bridge of the Golden Horn – I followed the torchlight that skipped on ahead.

A sinister aurora borealis up there, immediately above the Bazaar.

The stampede continues, the less robust dispersing along the way, continues through winding streets with treacherous potholes, heading toward the blaze.

There is a whole city of wooden houses burning irreparably.

Tonight the fire's share is a collection of houses. Tomorrow, who knows?

And they've even run from Scutari, passing through Bosphorus, because Scutari is also a town of mostly wooden buildings, it is the adjoining sister of Istanbul.

Sparks fall in bursts and and smoke whirls.

Police officers drive back imprudent curiosity with truncheon blows.

The fire grows in intensity.

The water hoses are too short and run badly as always, and the volunteer firefighters, the city's water carriers, start to pour the irony of a few buckets of water on the blaze.

Ah! these firefighters. I saw them in the morning, when, for a lack of fuel, the inferno faded away to ashes. I saw them returning, not with empty buckets, but with full ones – I'd say, booty.

The population rushes to the fire without losing a minute: solidarity, looting!

A strange country of contradictory outlines.

Turkey is paradoxical.

This is the absolute autocracy where the sultan wears the democratic fez instead of the crown.

Subversive philosophies emerge from simple facts.

In Constantinople, where thousands of dogs run free, rabies is still unknown. The skinny dogs of Galata have never bitten anyone. And you know why?

They have neither muzzles not masters!

## Spy

Despite the turbans, rare anyway around the fezzes, despite the discrete yashmak of the women, Constantinople, with its muddy streets, is not the Orient that you expect.

It is the East of Europe and that's all.

## The Long Trek

Will Asiatic Turkey perhaps be different? Certainly the same, with Damascus and Jerusalem, although in these necropolises the evocation should be specified.

But undoubtedly the hot vision of the Orient only breaks out on the shores bathed by the Indian Ocean.

Before leaving Constantinople, I wanted to visit Bosphorus and, volunteer tourist, dip my fingers into the Black Sea.

Such a large river, and sometimes a sudden bend, such a lake, a caldera surrounded by lush hills, Bosphorus stretches out and unrolls.

Under the sun, the villages along the way are jewels amidst the green: Therapia, Buyukdere, Kavaka.

Kavaka-Anatolia is the last village on the Asiatic coast before the tip of the strait. Cholera, which is rampant in Trabzon at this time, imposes a quarantine here on all who are coming from the Black Sea; passing through Kavaka would involve a sojourn in the quarantine hospital on the return trip – the ferry went no further.

On land, on the roads, or rather on the mountain paths that lead to the sea, a sanitary cordon has been established made up of soldiers on guard duty.

And the quarantine isn't the only thing one shouldn't violate; the particularly fortified place is, in fact, a strategic point that the Turks guard jealously.

Still I really want to go...

This desire to set foot for a moment on the shore of the Black Sea before turning back is probably a childish thing; but I feel it quite compellingly.[25] And since the paths are cut

---

25 The French here is "*tyranniquement*," that is, "tyrannically." I opted for

off, except for ravine that's considered impassable, I will take the path of the storm's rainwater.

The rugged slope is eroded, the stunted shrubs are uncertain support; I trickle down, clinging to branches and placing my feet on loose stones that frequently too courteously break away to accompany me. A half hour of these gymnastics with alternations between bouncing, scratching and wrenching; at the bottom of the ravine, I feel a positive relief.

This pleasant feeling doesn't last long. A sentry confronts me, calls out to me, shouts and raises his bayonet.

At his call, more soldiers rush over from a nearby cabin hidden in a thicket.

This is an alert for the post.

I can't make myself understood.

I get arrested.

A few hour later in Constantinople, where I was taken under a fine escort, they furnish me with an unexpected explanation: I was supposedly trying to evade the surveillance of the men on guard at a gunpowder storehouse at the Rumelia fortress.

My aim? espionage! …

A spy! And a Russian spy, if you please.

The thing would even delight me, if this had not perhaps been the origin of the misadventure that led me to write these lines in the leisure time of imprisonment.

After having persistently interrogated me in Russian, they tried French – everything was made clear.

---

a less literal translation that I felt made the point and sounded better in English.

But they demanded my papers.

I proved beyond a doubt that the government of my fatherland was on such terms with me that it could never be suspected of entrusting any mission to me.

Still, with the *incognito* broken, my identity established – probably drawing the attention of the French consul – I considered it most opportune to hasten my departure. I took the first ship calling at the Levantine ports.

My intention was to reach Jaffa; pushing into the land from there, I would visit Palestine.

Though I had ostensibly reserved a place for Jaffa, I hoped to set the alerted, ill-intended curiosity on the wrong track by not going there by a direct route. In fact, the chosen ship stopped in Mytilini, Smyrna, Chios, Rhodes, Cyprus, Beirut, and corresponded with other steamships on which my ticket would be valid for a whole month.

I would take this opportunity, for greatest enjoyment of my journey in love with shifting horizons.

On board, at the front, the bridge and the steerage had been taken over by Turks whose invading tribes had settled on mats, carpets and mattresses thrown haphazardly to immediately assert the taking of possession and the domain of each behind the border of boxes.

The ship was literally packed, and a feverish world was settling into a chirping of colors and voices.

A very narrow passage remained for circulating, and one would still have to carefully avoid tripping in the gridlocks.

I looked for a small spot to throw down my blanket for those nights.

It wasn't easy: the atmosphere seemed hostile to *Rŭm.*[26] And I had a noisy success when I boldly inserted myself in a narrow space left between a solemn rabbi with a corkscrew beard and three lovely and alarmed Armenian women... It took time for them to get used to it. And so as not to rush anything, at first I avoided looking at them too much.

From the place I'd conquered, standing, I focused on other unpredictables: the waves.

At the end of the Sea of Marmara, the Dardanelles bristle with their fortresses and cannons, and from Constantinople's other coast, Kavaka, the armed patrol boats on the Black Sea. We pass by Tenedos. We touch Mytilini (formerly Lesbos) – it became virtuous in its old age – and much less picturesque.

I stayed in Smyrna for a few days. Mosques and bazaars, a miniature Istanbul, with the additional characteristic of the cadenced march of camels in streets made of large stone slabs.

In fact, the city, with its houses covered with red tile roofs, doesn't amount to much aside from the ancient castle that dominates it: the castle of the Genoans, a superb ruin with broken down turrets.

Then there was Chios, Samos, the islands, groups of islands that seem to match each other with the great arms of their mills with white airfoils.

Rhodes, surrounded by crenelated walls; the old city closed, as if asleep, behind its Gothic gates; the Knight's Way, where there are houses decorated with chimaerical gargoyles they brought, engraved on the facade, coats of arms and insignias, crosses of Jerusalem and Malta. But if the Order left

---

26 A name Arabs used for the subjects of the Eastern Roman Empire.

## The Long Trek

a few traces, history turns into legend with regards to the famous Colossus. It is still to be learned where his bronze feet rested.

In Cyprus, warrior monks left few reminders aside from the dark red wines of the Commanderies.

The useless echoes of the past.

Further local characteristics: the English have put down roots.

You meet the redcoats, the roads are called *street* or *road*,[27] and I am drawn from my revery by a bicycle horn!

A few mornings later, the boat stopped at Beirut.

The sun rose gleaming in copper and gold on snowy Lebanon. And when I disembarked, I was again like one blinded. But my eyes quickly came back life in the light softened by canvas sheets stretched out on the sides of the streets. Further on, the coolness and shade under the stone arcades in the alleys, the coolness of the cellar and the damp greed shade of moss climbing up the arches.

It is the old quarter of Beirut.

There is also the modern city about which there is nothing to say, a section of the subprefecture with a bandstand and the road that stretches out in a dusty ribbon toward Damascus.

I had the displeasure of having to return to the ship too quickly; otherwise I would have had to wait a week for the next steamship that passed by: it was always a question of money!

As a spy, I am poorly maintained! Besides, now the closer I got, the more impatient I felt to land in Jaffa and direct my reconnaissance toward Jerusalem.

---

27 Here the italicized words are in English in the original.

## "Me consul"

Jaffa!

As the crew dropped anchor, a genuine flotilla of sturdy boats surrounded the steamship.

The flotilla danced to the whims of the choppy sea.

But the boats maneuvered so they could approach the ship's sides as closely as possible, and the boatmen shouted, gesticulated, strove to attract the attention of the passengers assembled in front, the fine pilgrims heading for Jerusalem, inexperienced travelers and not very calm, negotiating for their transport back to land.

Then, the anchoring maneuvers finished, as soon as the ladder was lowered, the boarding began with all the violence of that term: it seemed like an attack by corsairs.

The boatmen stampeded in the assault on the bridge. These huge hulks of men with bronze skin, bright clothing and bare legs, scattered in all directions, seizing baggage by force, cornering passengers, grabbing them by the clothes, dragging them, snatching them away from each other. And the insults, and the promises to charge less than their competitors, and the bewilderment of the meek pilgrims, and the panic.

I saw a venerable grandfather from Odessa holding tightly to the body of his young son who was being dragged willy-nilly toward one boat, while his wife was violently driven into another, and his young daughter, paralyzed with fear, let out heart-rending cries …

The captain, leaning calmly on the poop deck with some privileged first-class passengers, smiled, quite amused by the scene.

The world's poor were unloaded.

Now I threw myself into a full boat, and the tough boatmen still wanted to load up more. But we were tossed about by the waves so much that they decided to leave.

Five oarsmen rowed, standing, marking the strokes of the broad oars with a kind of guttural chant that sometimes grew wild like a cry of anguish when the largest waves hurled us from the heights into the deepest chasms.

We bounced while the boat's owner tried to fleece us: using the fierce weather as an excuse, he wanted to charge double, and right away. He went from one to another quite nimbly. One false move would have been enough to capsize us. A few weeks earlier, twenty-eight people drowned there – in what way – on the reefs.

Jaffa showed itself to be rather inhospitable.

We finally reached the steep coast.

I leapt.

I had barely set foot on the ground when a dozen men surrounded me: Turks and Levantines. They ordered me to follow them.

Where? I could see well where. I hesitated. They grabbed me.

Resisting would have been juvenile. Call the Turkish police? But they were there, approving, ready to give a strong hand.

I walked in the midst of this strange escort, and we went through the narrow paths of the steep slopes toward the upper city.

In short, what did I have to fear? Everything would be cleared up. Another adventure – and perhaps amusing.

We arrived at a large building where the French flag waved, and they told me:

"Here it is, come on, it's the hospital."

It was, in fact, the hospital. A nun, who was obviously forewarned, played host to me in the visiting room, where the chaplain and a Dominican missionary, wearing a fez, as noble as a caliph in the heavy folds of his white robe, already were. "Good day!" they said, and I waited, quite intrigued, in the silence of this staged scene.

A man entered suddenly like a gust of wind, with a gold-embroidered cap over his ear and a dog-whip in his right hand:

"Me consul arresting you."

What utter madness! What, that half savage creature, that grotesque being, gesticulating in front of me, represented France.

Our consul didn't speak my language…

I was arrested in pidgin French.

And why was I arrested? Why did they grab me there at the gates of Jerusalem?

The man explained to me in an exotic gibberish: he had orders.

All the consuls of the Levant had orders to seize me.

My coming had been announced.

In Port Said, In Alexandria, or in the barbaric provinces, the same thing would have happened to me: they had my description. They knew that I had been condemned for instigation to murder!

"You very bad," he concluded.

## He who trusts is crazy

Some individuals entered, armed, with braided uniforms, noisy.

The visiting room where the indigenous consul had notified me of the arrest was transformed into a police station.

The missionary and the chaplain remained there, silent, embarrassed – as indispensable witnesses. I congratulated them for their role. The hospital – perhaps state-funded? – had lent itself to the ambush …

Some dragomen in dress uniform, consular janissaries of a sort, came to frisk me.

They took my cash and papers, letters from friends, travel notes. They took away my bag in such a brutal way that for a moment I lost patience. I drove one of them back with a slap in the face.

In the brawl that followed was rough on my clothes, and my hat was smashed. I even lost an entire handful of hair. The personnel of the consulate dragged me through the institution's gardens to a pavilion where I was locked up in a room enforced with solid bars.

The singular diplomat with the amusing jargon came to taunt me behind the bars: I was quite wrong not to be satisfied. France is powerful in the Orient. This was all proper. I was arrested under the fine Capitulations. "The Capitulations", remember? … a treaty between the Sublime Porte and the great Francis I.[28]

---

28 Reference to the Capitulation signed by Francis I of France and Suleiman II the Magnificent. Turks used the term "the Sublime Porte" to describe the Ottoman government.

I stayed in that cell for fifteen days, in police custody. They chose the locale because they considered it more secure than the prison itself.

I was flatteringly surrounded by an abundance of safeguards.

The janissaries put up their tent not far from my room, and I could hear them late into the night, chanting their monotonous song. I always saw one of them passing back and forth in front of my window, armed with a gleaming scimitar.

Sometimes on the garden paths under the palms, I caught a glimpse of a white nun's cap that quickly vanished. They seemed like large birds frightened by a look.

The days passed all the same, long and without the illusion of a better tomorrow. My fate seemed all too clear to me. A ship was supposed to carry me away as soon as possible without further formalities.

It was an extradition.

Extradition for offenses of the press! Due to Francis I!

And in perspective, this was the mother country reopening its arms to me – its arms as prison gates.

## The Escape

The French mail boat was announced for the nest day, but the weather was so bad that the boat might not reach Jaffa. This would spending fifteen more days in the custody of the janissaries.

Night came without calming the winds that howled by, snapping off the long stems of the banana trees, and it must be breaking masts in the sea as well.

## The Long Trek

Despite the storm, the Turk on duty kept pacing around the pavilion – sword in hand!

It was only around eleven o'clock when, due to the torrential rain, the guard took refuge in the tent where his comrades were emptying their little cups of thick coffee for the twentieth time ...

Then, slowly, with a bar wrenched from the iron bed, I uncovered a hole in the wall that was once used for a stovepipe. This hole was carelessly blocked. I enlarged it. Occasionally a bit of rubble fell on the pavement, but the rain that kept falling and banging on the tent roof clearly deafened my guards.

I did it without hurrying, stopping at times to light up a cigarette.

I saw myself escaping.

Because this is it: the greatest amusements in life are the ones that we offer ourselves – a split personality of sorts. And I thought of other escapes without making a tragedy of this one. Especially curious.

I had dimmed the lamp that offered only a pilot light, and now, with the boldest blows, I attacked the breach.

The iron bar was alternately a crowbar or a battering ram that struck hard.

There was a huge crash: a collapse of copper and scrap iron. I was caught. Or maybe not. A brick falling into the adjacent room had knocked over a set of pots and pans, and still the men in the tent didn't move.

I was already able to risk sticking my head through the opening I'd made.

The adjoining space was a kind of kitchen-dining hall where the hospital's nuns must have dined. A bit more effort and the hole would be big enough for me to pass through.

It was already one o'clock in the morning.

But the dining hall door was locked; I had only changed cells! … Fortunately, one of the high windows didn't have bars, and I would only have to jump without making noise onto the soggy soil of the garden.

Ah! the first breath of fresh air. Despite the gusts of rain, what a feeling of joy. And also what amazement at my success. But not a final success, since the fence walls were proudly high.

I had trouble finding my bearings in the dark, which may have been made more unsettling by the single light beam given off by the lantern whose flame flickered in the tent.

Fumbling, stumbling, stopping suddenly, motionless, as I got mixed up with things, and then resuming the walk, I reached a shed where I found stacked wood. I climbed the piles, and, arms raised, I touched the top of the wall. My fingers were bloodied by broken bottles. Still I hoisted myself up and soon I was lying stretched out on the narrow ridge with scraped body and legs.

The street passed about fifteen to twenty feet below …

And I stayed there, in the downpour, taking a rest break.

The hospital was outlined as an imposing darker mass. I even made out the pavilion from which I had escaped, and below that, in the tent, I caught sight of the janissaries squatting in weary poses.

It was a strange spectacle.

Then I looked again at the long discreetly silent street. More than fifteen feet! It had to be done. And I let myself go, confident, to this lover: the highway.

The welcome was rough, and I was shaky when I stood up. But this passed with my first strides.

I was free.

## Jerusalem

I was wandering where chance took me on that stormy night.

I moved forward very quickly, thinking at times that I heard janissaries running in pursuit of me. But it was the sound of the wind blowing from the sea or the echo of my own footsteps in the sleeping city.

I was exploring Jaffa at a breathless pace, searching the shadows of the lower houses, rushing down the steep paths of the alleys, bombarding myself with a question: what should I do?

Gradually, the weather cleared. The rain stopped. The day was breaking, pale. I was on the steep rocks of the shoreline and caught sight of two large ships: a French ocean liner and a sailboat with the English flag. Salvation was there. But there were no boatmen on the coast and any native farmer was already at work. The dawn was full of threats.

What should I do?

A man spoke to me, but I didn't understand what he said.

At any moment, they might notice me and report me; a European can't wander around these parts without arousing attention. Besides, by this time the escape had certainly been discovered. The hunt was on.

I had to flee, and in a hurry.

I climbed up the steep bank of the city, which was shaped like an amphitheater.

This time I planned to get inside.

In the night's resting place, I had been able to glimpse Jerusalem, and, under the sky in which the star of the Magi had shone, chance might guide me to some unexpected refuge.

I went on.

I no longer hoped for an excursion along the Jordan and on the banks of the Dead Sea where Sodom and Gomorrah, debased societies, suffered the first propaganda of the deed.

Would I at least get into the Holy City? I focused my efforts toward that.

I moved forward tenaciously along uncertain roads.

And for a moment, I could imagine the eager anxiety of the Hebrews, so close – in vain – to the Promised Land.

## The Flag

By the time I reached the last houses, when I was finally setting out over the vast stretch of fine sand, on the caravan route, I came across a group of the native people who stared at me with suspicion in their eyes.

They were discussing, and I realized from their gestures that they were talking about me. When they were about one hundred feet behind me, they suddenly stopped.

Without turning my head, I felt their eyes fixed on me.

After a short consultation, the men turned around. They followed me at a brisk pace.

On the front of a building, an old faded sign marked the English consulate. The door was ajar.

I entered with a bound.

It was just in time: the men were coming at a run.

Closing the door behind me, I found myself in the presence of a worthy Semite who, despite the early morning hour, was hard at work, packaging with huge hammer blows.

His face, adorned with a glasses, remained calm.

I apologized.

He ushered me into an office of sorts, cluttered with gutted crates, register books, and cheap junk – a true smugglers' shambles.

On the whitewashed walls, amidst mildewed, fly-covered price lists and leaflets posters, there was a cheap color print of Queen Victoria.

My host, the worthy huckster, was the loyal consul of Her Gracious Majesty.

I had to take him into my confidence without enthusiasm.

He nodded without reaching a decision.

I continued, explaining that this corner of free territory was the most suitable refuge. British honor is at stake.

"If you only had money?" he insinuated cloyingly.

But since his colleague taken everything up to the buttons on my sleeves … He could do nothing, fearing difficulties. There was still Jaffa, where, aside from the French ocean liner where my place was reserved, there was an English boat. But it wasn't practical. There was still the question of money.

He bustled about evasively.

And while he continued to honor me with a few vague monosyllables, he went back to the waiting room, reopened the door, and went back to nailing crates.

No one was prowling around the building.

A good sign.

In disguise, at nightfall, it wouldn't be impossible to reach the English ship.

I would make arrangements with the captain.

Now I knew that the sailboat, which had come for a cargo of oranges destined for Glasgow, was supposed to make a stop in Gibralter.

Spain smiled on my journey with no itinerary.

Despite the welcome full of reservations, I was determined to wait there for the propitious moment. The ugly expression that the trader made ended up amusing me. I'd made up my mind.

I settled onto a parcel in the inviolable consulate.

I was tired and fell asleep.

It may have been around eight o'clock when loud yells woke me up. The consul had disappeared. A band of Turks wearing burnouses[29] had invaded the building.

I recognized two of my guards.

The gang seemed go be under the command of a dragoman from the French consulate who, for this glorious expedition, displayed a large tricolor rosette on his blue uniform with gold braids.

Oh! on these distant shores, the sight of the national colors!

The white-blue-red of the flag! Overcome with emotion, the eyes grow damp. Here is the protector, the great friend.

Like a vision of home.

Civilization, progress, people's rights. Proud memories. This is the chivalrous standard. Heart uplifted!

You play the barrel organ ...

---

29 A burnous is a long wide mantel, usually with a hood.

## The Long Trek

The chorus went out of fashion. Passengers carried about by the Cook Agency are the only ones left to perpetuate the curious species of bipeds that the tricolor causes to weep. In the midst of scenic landscapes, closer to Nature, sensitive people can better perceive the banality of the Flag. In countries with magical scenery, it is an anti-joy[30] for the eye.

It is a gaudy piece of cloth with an Epinal[31] aesthetic style.

And let's talk from the heart. All the vagabonds, chased across the world because they thought out loud, are not like whipped dogs who love the cudgel. They have been beaten mercilessly with the pole of the symbolic banner – and they understand.

And though they don't hiss at the flag, they despise it.

Civilization, progress, people's rights. The inviolable refuge has been violated. The individual with the rosette jumped me, an insult on his lips; his henchmen seized me and pushed me out of the consulate.

I stopped struggling, very disgusted, thinking: Too bad!

The triumphant Franco-Turks hounded me, fists on my back. We plummeted down a precipice toward the shore.

The crowd swelled behind us, and when we stopped at the boats, the whole population thronged the narrow coast.

The nervous grasps didn't let loose of me; they gripped the flesh under my clothing. Ten men clung to me superstitiously, as if, through some mysterious spell, I might still escape.

---

30 "*Contre-joie*" in French. The implication seems to be that in a place where the environment is beautiful, the flag is a blot on that beauty, an eyesore.

31 A city in southern France, famous for the production of popular images and prints.

Then the French consul arrived, out of breath.

He gave his connoisseur's approval and, what's more, had my legs shackled.

What were they waiting for to put an end to it, say the final word and take me on board?

The consul became solemn.

He was waiting for something that should already be there, but that, at least, he had to see in the boat for the fugitive's transport – something indispensable.

Something official.

I waited for this something for three quarters of an hour, booed by a motley rabble.

They went quite far in search of this something, to the other end of the city, to the consulate:

It was the flag.

## For Murderers

They threw me to the bottom of the boat.

The dragomen tied me up so tightly that it was difficult to breathe and also attached me to the seat. One of them sat at the back, holding the consulate's flag that flapped in the wind. The short, rough, agitated waves crashed and shattered, turning white on the red reefs. We moved forward, tossed by the breakers along the way.

I can guarantee that in such instances you look at the rocks without pleasure and have foolish apprehensions in finding yourself tied up this way.

And besides, this way of traveling, wrapped up in a tangle of rope, has a thousand and one inconveniences, the last of which is that of making ... an ugly impression on others. So, when they set me down, like a slightly fragile package, aboard the French ocean liner, the crew gave me sidelong looks. The officer of the watch took me into custody.

In a lovely, completely military spirit, he immediately untied me, returned the ropes that I had been wrapped in to their rightful owners, and pointed me out to his sailors, giving the order: "Stick him in irons."

The apparatus is rather simple: a bar equipped with two movable rings that serve as bracelets for the feet. The best position when you wear such jewelry is horizontal. It's good to stretch out on your back, so that you avoid movements that cause abrasions on the ankles. During the pitching and rolling this wouldn't be easy.

Could you perhaps get used to it?

I did my training on the bridge, in front.

This ancient torture of the bar was revived with another singularly modern punishment. The passengers and sailors came in a procession to gape at me.

They treated me like an animal in a trap.

They inspected and examined me. I was left at the mercy of their perverse malice, like someone on the pillory.

I sympathized with the miserable murderers nabbed in overseas cities for whom these various tortures are the rule. What a desperate return. How long the days must be, passed under the implacably inquisitive eyes of the onlookers. How nagging those hours are in which no one has the compassion to leave them alone for even one moment – alone with their dejection. Oh! Why not put them in the hold, these unfortunates! A dark dungeon, if you will; but not the anguish of irons on the bridge. Why, why brutally aggravate the ordeal of the guillotine?

Of course, the misfortune wasn't such a big thing for me, since I wasn't going back to Deibler[32]. It struck me, most of all, in teaching me about the barbarities more and more in use, against which those given over to the executioner, those who suffer these barbarities, have no time to protest. Perhaps its not so bad that from time to time these barbarities accidentally strike someone who can denounce them.

I have earned the right to protest in favor of the human cattle who are led, under torture, to the national slaughterhouse.

No doubt, I should also say that the cruelest incidents can produce unusual sensations that are not completely unpleasant to experience.

Every reverse has its coin.

And besides, everyone should know how to live through what mere criminals suffer, if need be.

All this was really just a rather heavy farce.

I straightened up, sitting on the damp, slippery deck, and turned my head away from the voyeurs.

The cabin boy jokers were not the most relentless.

The most relentless were the tourists who passed by, talking among themselves in low voices and feigning contempt and disgust. An Englishman, wearing a white helmet with a green veil, approached. He gave his arm to a lady who

---

32 Anatole Deibler, perhaps the most famous executioner, executed 395 people condemned to death on the guillotine between 1890 and 1939, after five years training as his father's assistance.

smiled with her long teeth at the entertainment not foreseen on the program.

"Villain, what did you do?" the gentleman asked me.

I chanted clearly in a solemn voice:

"I cut an old woman up into thirteen pieces, and it gave me a migraine."

## At Sea

The French ship, "*La Gironde*" of the maritime Freight Service, where I was housed with so little comfort, was heading for Marseilles via Port Said and Alexandria.

As we left the dock, the wind died down.

The day was calm, the evening warm – one of those evenings when everyone gathers on deck.

The presence of a chained man on the forecastle had been mentioned up as far as the first-class table. Someone had probably repeated my name. And after dinner, a very elegant man of about fifty years, with a flowing beard, came to visit me, quite enraged.

"I know who you are!" he yelled.

He got worked up, gesticulated, incited the other passengers, saying I was a kind of anarchist and the the best thing would be to throw me overboard:

"Into the water, anarchist!"

In his comical excitement as a ferocious bourgeois, he reviled me with nonsense and with such a huge barrage of hilarious epithets that I responded with bursts of laughter.

It was certainly not the time to expand upon the Idea that is dear to my heart and that the word anarchy can only roughly explain.

My attitude pushed the old fellow's rage to its limit. His friends had to drag him away by force, for fear that he would have a stroke.

The next day, when we reached Port Said, the distinguished madman disembarked with different baggage.

The captain, informed of the man's ridiculous escapade, showed his dissatisfaction by having my irons removed … He was baffled that a person could provoke a defenseless individual.

But isn't that always the story?

An innocent, a fine man, that captain, rugged and kindly, who had sailed the Chinese seas for ten years of his life. He gave me a cabin, granted me permission to move about at my own pleasure, and when he noticed that my hat – damaged by the janissaries – was rather odd, extended me his courtesy by offering me a felt hat that hadn't been through such a war.

I kept that gray felt hat, the hat of the good captain!

A beautiful, ten-day voyage on this large lake, under the blue sky. I forgot for hours on end, through bits of starry night, that I was sailing toward jail. Alexandria, always young, at the forward edge of the pyramids, purplish-blue Crete on the horizon, the iridescent panorama of the sea, the renewed joys of free travel.

I would have to give it up.

At the foot of the Calabrian mountains, in a vision of wild nature, I sensed the irony of my situation most bitterly.

Toward evening, in the Strait of Messina, where Etna snores in her sleep, we followed the Italian coast. The fishing boats surrounded the ship. You could see the peasants in the villages returning from the fields. When I saw the

## The Long Trek

coast so close, a bitter desire gripped me, a wish to plunge toward the shore, toward freedom, and to reconquer it by swimming.

But too many people were watching on board, leaning over the rails, attentive to the views, and the night was not yet dark.

Did I have the scruples of a prisoner on parole?

Perhaps.

So many prejudices that no longer hamper our minds, still paralyze our actions.

We hesitate.

What some have called a point of honor is transposed into a matter of conscience.

To avoid any trouble for the exceptional jailer who is a good man, you give up, without struggle, the only good that makes existence worthwhile.

The defeated have the currency for the latest market of dupes.

The moment passed. It was no longer possible to try anything.

The rustic coast disappeared.

We left the strait that opened grimly between the rocks of Scylla and Charybdis.

But soon the Mediterranean regained its look of an attractive beguiler. Day and night, its charms soothe you. We passed the island of Sardinia. And on a clear morning, we saw Marseilles rising before us.

As soon as the ship docked, hugging the banks of Joliette, two characters in overcoats came onto the footbridge and called for the captain. He presented me to them without delay.

The first, an agent of the Ministry of the Interior, was charged with telling me that my arrest in Jaffa was not considered legal.

Consequently, he released me.

The other, in the service of Justice, only added:

"Yes, but since you are here, I have the duty to arrest you."

## Black Sheep

They took me to a large courtyard where about forty men walked back and forth or squatted in small groups in the spots where they could catch the sun.

A guard with an inquisitor's eye fingered the noisy rosary of a set of keys.

My arrival caused a certain sensation: the others surrounded the new arrival. There was a deluge of questions. How much time did he get? What did he do? Fraud or blackmail? A small job with a knife?

They even brought up rape.

The prisoners demanded my credentials. Was I part of the underworld or did I operate the hard way? I answered: "It depends …"

This wise response earned me the approval of an old repeat offender who saw himself as my buddy. He led me away from the others and told me:

"Old boy, beware!"

"How's that?"

"Well, if you have anything in your pocket – your dough or tobacco? – someone will swipe it from you. You'd do best to entrust it to me. Between men of the world there's an understanding. I was a notary twelve years ago …"

"Ah!"

"And then I see well," he added, changing tone, "my dear sir, my dear, dear sir, I see well that we will understand each other. These people are not of our sort. They are scoundrels. I'll tell you my story. I am innocent."

And the fellow went on to tell me his troubles in detail.

He was a little old man with the cunning look, the prancing speech, the gestures of a robber, a curious type of professional.

He must have had adventures that weren't too mundane.

He was an artist of a sort, and I liked to imagine him in colorful "cons".

But he only thought of exonerating himself. To hear him, he was an honest petty bourgeois who was hounded by malicious enemies. He had always respected the law:

"It is sacred, my dear sir."

He willingly spoiled his style, disowning his life. The old freebooter became a shameful thief. I started to despise him. A kind of athlete with a fierce look joined us.

"He's a friend," my companion said. "The poor fellow hasn't had any luck either."

"Oh! sir, if you knew," the other said. "It's unfair! My boss threw himself on a knife – a knife that I accidentally had – and wounded himself. Is that my fault? Well! They sentenced me to six months! It's unfair! But I have my honor all the same. I am not a scoundrel. I don't attack bosses, not I, sir."

Other prisoners approached us; we walked slowly around the courtyard, a bit too close to each other, and the walk was getting on my nerves in any case. Most of these men posed as victims without rancor.

They instinctively bowed to Authority, Property, Law.

All these outcasts hung their heads.

Even the ones who confessed to a theft – the theft of a pair of shoes or a ham from a shop window when they had an empty belly and bare feet – looked for an excuse.

They pretty nearly spoke well of the police. And when one lone street urchin, arrested, I believe, for vagrancy, yelled, "Ah! no, I'm fed up with the pigs!", an honest pickpocket, with everyone's approval, peremptorily answered him:

"But, in the end, we have to have the police!"

Finally, in the face of these ugly, humiliated posturings, I stopped hiding my disgust. Had they taken me for a "gentleman", perhaps a shady businessman in bankruptcy, but still a man of principles, and is this why they played at being goody-two-shoes?

Well, then, they really missed the mark.

I quickly explained to them that honesty consists solely in being frank with yourself, that you have to claim responsibility for your actions. That if you don't feel that you acted as an idiot or a madman, but rather with awareness, you should proudly proclaim:

"I did this for this and that reason, because I needed it, and no one would give me a hand, because I was exploited and my exploiter made a fool out of me.

"I did this and I did it well.

"This is honor."

The guard had come up, and now he shouted at me, "Hey! the big man spouts off. Your comrades aren't excited. Would you care to shut up? ... Who are you to look me over? ... Come with me to the warden."

I followed him to the head guard and the matter was quickly resolved.

"What!" the chief said harshly, "Here there are undoubtedly a few unfortunates who acted badly – it is easy to make a bad shot; but these fellows aren't completely rotten. They have some recourse ... And you corrupt them for me. Go on! Into the cell!"

And this is how I, the criminal writer, was separated from the "common law" prisoners.

## The Last Hotel

After a month in the Marseilles prison, two new-model cops, with patent leather boots and top hats, escorted me to Paris.

For them, it was a golden opportunity, the chance to spend a day or two on our boulevards – small Cannebières[33]!

The pleasure they expected from this put them in jovial mood.

They were almost grateful to me: if I listened to them, I would dine with them at the Lyons buffet.

We separated at the transit prison.

Three days later, I entered Sainte-Pélagie.

Ten political prisoners lived acrimoniously in the Pavilion of Princes.

I was the eleventh.

---

33 Cannebière is the main avenue of Marseille, often compared to the Champs-Élysées in Paris.

To announce the arrival of a letter or a visitor, the bell that sounded once for our doyen, sounded eleven times for me!

But soon, as someone's prison time ended, it would sound ten times, then nine. … Some pardons were granted, and the same day a whole bunch was granted conditional liberty. Two strokes now designated my level. Then the doyen ceded his place to me and his room that had the biggest window. I was the oldest – at a single stroke! – and for a long time.

Alas! How I saw prisoners leaving.

Even those I had seen come in, soon replaced, short sentences – jokes! Though one was macabre and sinister: the bouncing ball game that the poor Gardrat was forced to suffer in agony, lugged from Pélagie to Santé and back again.

Thirty years old, with a B.A. degree, Gardrat had gallantly accepted the editorship of a journal precisely when the editors-in-charge were hard to find, when the first judiciary actions accusing us of "criminal association" began.

The sentence wasn't slow in coming.

He took refuge in London, and then came back, pushed by poverty that earned him his first coughing fits in the cold nights spent on the benches in Hyde Park.

He was arrested in Paris, and the dampness of the cells in the Conciergerie continued the work. The penitentiary administration finished it.

It was painful to see the unfortunate lad in Sainte-Pélagie. So desperately frail, he dragged himself up the steep staircase of the ancient monastery. He came down gasping for breath, struggling, shaken by the crises that made him stop at the landings, with his throat contracted and his mouth gaping. It was for air, for air that he called, and he had vaguely hoped to catch his breath just now in the sad, sunless courtyard …

So many times we carried him back up in our arms, his poor body, oh! so painfully light.

Fed up with his daily visits, the prison doctor had Gardrat transferred to Santé's infirmary, where the disciplinary regime was such that he was kept from sending me his news for several days. But his complaints led to his return to Sainte-Pélagie.

He returned to us spitting out his life.

That was in June. On July 14, the administration decided to remember Gardrat.

On that national feast day, they sent him back to Santé!

A heart-breaking event occurred.

They took advantage of an early morning hour, when we were still in bed, to take him away. It was in the paddy wagon, I can't say how he got in – he could no longer do it himself – but they hoisted him up, already dying.

A bit later, we learned that they had cut up his body, his pitiful, tortured body, on an autopsy table.

There it is, death lies in wait for young men.

Twice in less than a year, it was the prison's guest.

Another prisoner, Jean Lécuyer, whose odyssey was similar to that of Gardrat spent his time till nearly his last day in the "great tomb", the dark cell.

When the end was already near, they granted him an ironic liberty – the freedom to go die in a hospital. As one of the administration doctors told the sick man himself in his most engaging voice: "You wouldn't believe how much trouble a death causes here. It never ends: observations, forms to fill out, derogatory comments. In the hospital, on the other hand, you go by yourself."

And you go more quickly! Jean Lécuyer didn't last more than fifteen days.

We seem so far from the legendary times when people in Pélagie laughed.

Even when nothing tragic happens, there is the dismal stagnation of warriors not ready for the cloister. All these prisoners, whose customary crime is loving freedom too much, champ at the bit in the forced inactivity of the hybrid prison into which echoes from the outside penetrate, inciting them.

The instinct for battle suppressed, diminished, the rough edges of the personality stirred, it makes useless quarrels and childish malice.

No, Sainte-Pélagie is not the fraternal academy of a rebel philosophy, something like the Villa Medici of malcontents. I remember it, in Rome, the Villa where I spent many hours in the workshop of good friends. "It is our Sainte-Pélagie, for ourselves," they said.

They were wrong. Here, even more than there, you lose the fine enthusiasm for effort. Perhaps the analogy exists only in the less seductive aspects: Sainte-Pélagie is the gossip house of Pot-bouille.[34]

I won't go into the mundane details of a banal existence where at times, not to chatter on, you play dice games all day

---

34 This is the title of a novel by Emile Zola published in 1882. In the 19th century, the term commonly referred to the domesticated pig. But Zola used it metaphorically to refer to the back side of a large Parisian building, where behind a luxurious façade lived some bourgeois families whose daily behavior was as disgusting as mediocre pigswill.

long ... the visiting room hours with a guard in the corner, and night when nine o'clock tolls, the arrival of the turn-key who makes the monumental locks of our rooms squeak.

And what is there to say about the letters subjected to the censor's stamp and the blood-red, zigzagging initials of the warden, which grace the newspapers after they've been examined – even the *Temps* itself!

A few words furtively exchanged with common prisoners, the "orderlies" who sweep the stairs.

I hear ugly stories and learn that the guards, fairly polite with us, are cruel on the other side.

Every day, dozens of men feed on hard bread. In the winter there is no heat, and you are punished in damp dungeons.

You come out of there crippled, rheumatic consumptive.

In the workshops, there is a shameless traffic, from five thirty in the morning until seven thirty in the evening, without stop! Except for one hour that includes both meals, of meager broth.

And what do the most skillful earn?

Sixty centimes[35] an hour – half for the administration.

Most others get only two or three pennies.

It is true that, for example, for those purses – they even teach you how to make change purses! – for those purses that normally cost one franc and forty-five centimes, the prisoner is paid twelve centimes.

And the punishment units!

Though Clichy no longer exists, it's even worse. The smallest infraction leads to bodily constraint, so that even

---

35 Back in the 1960s, when I was a kid, this would have been the equivalent of about 12 to 15 cents.

individuals who haven't yet been sentenced are consigned to the prison regime.

At times, you hear the steps of these punishment units passing by, with the wooden clogs that echo rhythmically in the paved courtyard. They call it "the sausage". They march in single file, on command: left, right, left!

This is the modern way to atone for the crime of poverty …

Why go on about the small annoyances that we ourselves suffer in this prison which, for us, is really a sort of poorly-kept hotel with a surly innkeeper, while a stifled and painful moan rises from the annex.

This moan is what we need to expose.

We need to track the regime's morality with factual evidence. One prisoner (S., #986) came to do one year of prison.

In this time, he did four days in solitary confinement for chatting in the workshop.

A month before his release, he asked the warden for permission to grow his beard, so that he wouldn't have to leave with his bare face as the bald notification of his sojourn in prison.

Request refused, because he had been punished.

Such refusals are everyday occurrences.

Some people are physically prevented from going back to work in this way. They bear a mark. They don't dare present themselves or are poorly received. And then? …

Another prisoner who had one day of dry bread in a six months sentence (his first conviction) couldn't get permission either. It's worth reflecting on the response of the prison's

Ramollot[36]: "Next time, when you return, you will try to behave better."

Sad times when nothing moves anymore, when the mass is inert, when writers take no risks.

Resigned acceptance tarnishes Paris.

From "Great Siberia", the last cell at the top, where the view extends over the city, I ponder with my head against the bars, while the houses are gloomy in the half-mourning of their gray façades. The flabbiness that has replaced the superb unruliness of a people shows me a city in lethargy.

Who will sound the wake-up call?

Paris seems like a necropolis. Or, more inexorably, like a jail. And in the lucid mirage of a view, at the horizon, all the windows have the same bars as my window.

And down below, beneath the Pitié hospital, beyond Mazas, to the right and below the July Column where the genius of Liberty perpetually seems to be chained to the enormous ball – in the distance, a somber green hill: the Pére Lachais cemetery.

The monument to the executioner Thiers[37] casts a sour note like an invocation next to the concession of Casimir-Périer[38].

---

36 A reference to colonel Ramollot, a character invented by the writer Charles Leroy in 1883. He is the embodiment of the old soldier: stupid, violent, brutalized by the service.

37 Adolphe Thiers (1797-1877), chief executive from 1871-1873, was responsible for the repression of the Paris Commune.

38 Jean Paul Pierre Casimir-Périer, son of one of Thiers' cabinet ministers, held several institutional posts, and then became Council President and Minister of Foreign Affairs under the presidency of Sadi Carnot,

Then at the top of the little hill, there is the chimney of crematorium furnace. That morning, in the raging wind, a light smoke suddenly swirled. This is when the body of our fellow prisoner, Lécuyer, burned.

The tiny white puff of smoke swirled, rose and dispersed …

---

between December 3, 1893 and May 23, 1894. He was the architect of the infamous "black laws", which struck at individual freedom and so-called crimes of the press. He was elected President of the Republic on June 27, 1894, following the assassination of Sadi Carnot by the anarchist Sante Caserio. A few months later, in December, the scandal of the Dreyfuss affair broke out. Having become uncomfortable, Casimir-Périer resigned on January 16, 1895 and retired from political life.

*Chapter 5*

# FROM BOTH SIDES

## Through the Bars

MORNING VISITORS ARE BECOMING RARE IN THE VISITING room. It's amusing to come visit the prison once, almost like going on a tour of the rebuilt Bastille. Once, not twice.

And then, Sainte-Pélagie is so far away ...

At times, I wonder, but without worry, if someone is spreading unfortunate rumors about me, if someone has discovered some crooked action for which they are holding me liable, if the silence of one-time associates springs from honest reservations.

But that's not it.

A year and a half is a long time. It is a death. and you don't even go to the grave.

But I'll come out of it alive enough.

And without bitterness against the failures of camaraderie. They are doing me a favor. Sometimes on the street, in chance encounters, in the banalities exchanged, you almost imagine that you aren't walking alone. And this small blow to vanity that, in prison, shows you how very quickly you are forgotten is healthy. It is a good thing. It makes you stronger.

Isolation echoes this: we exist only for ourselves.

In these times of debilitating geniality, the fewer relationships you have with men of letters, the better it is. Fraternal and free-masonic antics are also bonds.

Let's smash them!

To speak clearly and without restraint: Know as few people as possible! You feel lighter, surer.

Down through the months, I sifted out comrades.

Certain loyalties proved sufficient. Friends remain. And I know how involved life is, how difficult and demanding. Do I have to add that the latest hunters for "malefactors" locked those I love best up in Mazas? These are the ones I miss the most. I bear imprisonment better than those who knew me might have thought.

My passion for freedom reasons: am I significantly less free here than in life in this country, where you are forbidden openly speak your mind? I've reflected on it. I work a bit. And am I any worse off in my cell, where I isolate myself, and feel no more offended than in the midst of the unaware crowds of the July 14[39] and the Russian celebrations?

It is also like a prison on the other side of the bars.

A growing contempt for the emptiness that is now called the citizen's freedom leaves you with less regret when you hear republican locks latching behind you. This is nothing

---

39 Bastille Day the primary French patriotic holiday.

but the materialization of a slavery that you may feel more strongly in the unveiled spectacle that life outside of prison imposes.

Independence now is only for the mind. And I keep this independence here despite the jailer.

For most human beings in the social mechanism, freedom is just a word with no purpose.

You don't breather deeply, you vegetate.

You struggle, you eat poorly, and you no longer think.

The life of a beast! always, everywhere, cramped, petty, ugly. From my window, looking over the street at an angle, I have the Lame Devil's[40] intrusive view of a whole block of apartments.

Everyone seems bored, barely alive.

Even the couple that comes back every evening to dine, with the table well spread in front of the two geraniums on the window sill.

The table cloth is white.

Habitually, they always put the bread, the butter, the salt in the same place, the liter of wine on the little wooden coaster.

They are meticulous, even anxious, skittish, with furrowed brow. The husband, most likely a commercial employee, can't shake off the torpor of his empty day. The woman works twelve hours in a shop.

---

40 A reference to Alain-René Lesage's novel *The Lame Devil* (also known as *The Devil on Two Sticks*), in which the demon, Asmodeus, takes the young student, Cleotus, on a flight over Madrid, uncovering the roofs of the houses to show him the inhabitants and tell him their secrets.

Just like at work, they always appear on time before the well-set table.

The weighed, silent, mechanical punctuality of their existence gives an automatic *je ne sais quoi*[41] air in the midst of the familiar order of objects.

But the other evening, they were more animated, something that they didn't quite understand seemed to disturb their customary harmony.

Their gestures were impatient, their eyes searching.

The man noticed it first: the little coaster was missing under the liter of wine.

They argued for two hours …

Now I imagine this clerk who spends his day performing his boring job behind the grid of a counter.

I am more free behind these bars!

I could achieve a calm indifference through disgust, if a tenacious hatred didn't awaken at the reading of the domesticated newspapers that daily report some new roguery, miscarriage of justice, abuse of power, insults to those defeated by fate and in revolt.

I like to look closely, it's good to point out the lackeys and bosses, the true criminal association: bribes, news stories, secret funds.

People endure it in compulsory silence.

We'll make up for the silent days.

Months and months go by here. I did well not to sign the

---

41 "*Je ne sais quoi*" is a French phrase that is also used in English (and other languages) to refer to a quality that can't be easily described or named. It most literally translates as "I don't know what".

petition for a pardon when it was suggested to me, with the assurance of a good reception.

It was just a trap. In fact, I am one of the few not to benefit, at half the penalty, from this parole, which is, so they say, due by right.

After so many others, one of our comrades has just left thanks to the application of this law, and so there are just two of us in the large structure where we wander around like ghosts ...

I'm not complaining. When I went back to the Court of Assizes on my return from Jaffa, my second crime, noticeably less innocuous than the first, only cost me six additional months of punishment, that was then remitted most likely due to the scandal caused by my extra-legal arrest. In short, it's only eighteen months which are now on the wane. Happily, I see the end coming ... My last faithful visitors will be in for a surprise. They will find a change in the visiting room, that big, bare room where four sparse seats represented comfort. It is nearly a living room now – and what style!

I expect a cry of joyful surprise. The cry isn't slow in coming. At the sight of the large antique oak table, the long benches with back rests, benches from a workshop or a monastery, the friends who came to find me that afternoon, my old collaborators, exclaim and cheer: they have recognized ... the furniture of the paper's office.

In Sainte-Pélagie, they again find themselves in our editorial room.

Then we sit around the table that police inspector Clément raided so many times, looking for dynamite in the pen cases. The good old suspect table! the good friend, what fate! But also that beautiful appearance, severe, shining and well polished, at the center of the visiting room, under the respectful eye of the guard.

It was necessary, due to a notice to leave, to move out of our cellar in rue Bochard de Saron, which after the paper's forced eclipse, was only used as a dormitory for homeless comrades. The owner refused to renew the lease.

It was his right. And, according to tradition in Sainte-Pélagie, it was my right to get some office furniture for my cell.

Drumont had furnished his room, and I was allowed the same liberty. It's just that the huge table and large benches couldn't fit through my door, so they remained in the visiting room and now ...

We are at home.

A stimulating reappearance. For awhile, my friends would say: "We're holding our ground."

Isn't this the honor of war?

We are modest. And we remember when the organ – sold, alas! in the collapse – resounded under the arches of our cellar, when we no longer lacked copy.

If it weren't for the guard in his corner, we would have forgotten the prison.

*L'Endehors* is in its furniture!


## False Exit

Coincidences express themselves with malice.

So, I was arrested far away, on January 1, 1893, the same day that the impenitent Anton[42], under the watchful eye

---

42 L. E. Anton was implicated in the Panama Canal scandal as one of

of agent Dupas, was luring pigeons on San Marco plaza in Venice. I was released on July 1, 1894, the day of Carnot's burial. So that day of national mourning and official weeping promised to be a happy day for me.

I'm ashamed.

It would have been justice if a cloud had darkened my joy.

The cloud wasn't slow in coming, heavy and filthy. It took the form of group of police keeping watch at the gate of Sainte-Pélagie, who advanced like a storm cloud as soon as I set foot on the sidewalk.

To start with, arresting someone who has just spent eighteen months under the care of the prison administration is disconcerting; but accusing him of being part of a criminal association as well becomes a serious and plausible matter, when you recall that in prison you are forced to associate with the prison warden.

Since they had stopped me at the door before I had pulled it shut, there was just one thing I could do:

A step back.

I made it. And I took refuge with my accomplice.

The guard-doorkeeper, who did not forcibly oppose my reentry, was probably later quite harshly rebuked.

---

the main perpetrators of political corruption, and his name was mentioned frequently in parliamentary debates and in the press. Though he was officially investigated, the authorities didn't try to catch him until 1895, when he was arrested in London. Consequently extradited and convicted in 1896, in the confessions he made in prison, he accused at least 104 members of parliament involved in the Panama affair. All the accused were quickly tried and exonerated of all accusations in 1897. In 1898, Anton was pardoned in his turn.

In fact, the situation was quite bizarre:

A freed prisoner, who has been released from custody, whose name has been struck from the books, whose departure has happened, and who is still there, like a recalcitrant tenant determined not to get evicted.

I went back into to my cell, quickly burned certain papers that compromised my suitcase, and waited …

It didn't take long.

Eight local soldiers, their sergeant, the warden, and two key-keepers – an imposing force – came to order me to leave.

I graciously yielded to these uniformed bailiffs, these kindly French soldiers, who had no idea what was happening and swayed like silly beasts, looking in astonishment at the flames in the fireplace that had nearly finished consuming the last bits of paper. The police were still waiting patiently at the door.

I changed escorts, and we went to the nearest police station, the one in rue Cuvier, at the corner entrance of the Botanical Garden.

The sergeant on duty, an old man with a suspicious eye, couldn't look at my fluttering tie without worrying; to avoid responsibility for a suicide with a floppy neck tie, he confiscated it.

So my entry into the lock-up took place in the wrong attire.

It's true that no one noticed this in the dark, stinking hole into which they pushed, since my cellmates were three drunks concerned solely with flooding the area with smelly hiccups.

Later, they brought an acquaintance of mine, Le Père Lapurge[43], well-known in the Latin Quarter for not very

---

43 Literally, "Father Purge". His given name was Constant Marie. He was

mundane songs in which the word dynamite exploded in the chorus.

Le Père Lapurge was a bald, plump bricklayer, with a calm rosy face.

He's so peaceful and gentle.

Looking like a small shopkeeper from Marais – he terrorized the neighborhood of the Pantheon.

I had just asked him to sing me one of his explosive ballads, when a police officer came to get me.

The police commissioner wanted to see me.

"Well! You won't be leaving," he said briskly, "and the cell in rue Cuvier is not like Sainte-Pélagie. Oh! Certainly not. It smells bad. So, do you want to stay in the police station? We don't grant such favors to everyone. But no tricks. Do I have your word, eh?"

"What a question, Mr. Commissioner! You know who I am …"

"But, yes, of course. I also used to write for newspapers. I know how it is."

And quite superior and sympathetic, with a protective gesture, this friend of the press walked away.

Sitting on the wooden bench by the office, I waited for hours, listening to the officers who occasionally returned, talking about the funeral:

"Oh my! There was so much sunstroke. I took three guys to Pitié."

"My old man, you should have seen the parade of firefighters from Chatou. splendid!"

---

an anarchist and a poet who had been active in the Paris Commune. He wrote a number of revolutionary songs.

"There were three floats full of flowers. How chic!"

"All the streets are blocked; the paddy wagon won't get here before nightfall."

"So who are the people in the parade wearing berets and breeches?"

"That I don't know. There are some of every type. There are some with plumed hats, boots, and great coats. There are others in hunting costumes, but without the horns."

"You haven't seen anything if you didn't notice the guys with cocked hats and yellow uniforms."

"What do those fellows represent?"

"They're the delegation of husbands!" the sergeant bellowed, pounding the table.

They laughed uproariously. They had never more loudly agreed with the sergeant. They doubled up with laughter.

Now the police talked about the "cavalcade".

"It is what makes you thirsty!"

And all these men, with their white gloves and the mourning bands on their arm, gave the irresistible impression of carnival undertakers.

Poor Carnot, such sick weeping!

If they didn't think of the dead, they cared even less about me.

After drinking, the officers went out to take some air in front of the police station.

It was the moment.

There was an window in front of me, brightened with nasturtiums, that opened onto the Botanical Garden. I climbed quickly through a leafy circle and made my way at a run along the path.

A thin wire mesh fence of rusted steel and the sound of my fall gave the alarm.

"Stop him!"

I fled more quickly amidst the surprise of Sunday strollers.

"Stop him!"

A howling mob had already formed behind me. I perceived the flowering of a timid cruelty, growing bolder bit by bit.

The mob was roused and set in motion.

Everyone.

And everywhere.

Little by little, the cry swelled, a confused rumble that was sharpened now with women's shouts, until some children threw their rope between my legs.

I was abruptly stopped and, unfortunately, at an outlet that opened right onto the path that led to the police station, a hundred yards further on.

"Stop him! stop him!"

It was the killing cry. I had to run in a straight line while up ahead, men massed to block the street, called by the shouts.

An individual stood in front of me with outstretched arms:

"No one passes here!"

I responded by punching the wannabe-cop in the face, as the crowd shouted even more loudly:

"Stop him, he's an anarchist!" The people couldn't be at all mistaken. The wanna-be cop was shabbily dressed, and they took him for the anarchist!

With heart-touching unity, they beat the living daylights out of the courageous citizen.

"But it's not me," he pleaded.

From Mazas to Jerusalem

It was no use. And it all happened so fast, and with such gusto, that the guy was half dead when the police arrived.

"It's not me, it's not me," he repeated, clinging to my jacket.

"Shut up, you," the officer said, as his face puffed up, "you are more guilty than him."

In the confusion, these drunken brutes thought that the poor over-zealous creature had tried to help my escape ... At the same time, I was seized, and quite rudely led back to the police station.

The shameful lynch mob shouted as we passed and formed a line shaking fists and canes with a hysterical desire to deal anonymous blows.

Cowardly people!

And they aimed for the wounded man!

My safeguard was in being in one piece and better dressed, head high with a sure look. A single false step and I would have been treated like the other.

I didn't even go back to the police station. The paddy wagon had just arrived, and I sped off to the transit prison, while the good citizen took my place, getting locked up in the cell.

## On the Street

Should I say: from Mazas to Jerusalem—and back (via Marseilles, Sainte-Pélagie and the transit prison)? I may consider it. On the occasion of Carnot's funeral[44], I found a handful of comrades in prison; they get arrested at every celebration including May Day.

These festivals usually end for them in Mazas.

But the warden called me almost immediately:

I am free.

The idiotic police arrested me too soon. They overstepped their order, which was to leave me at least a few hours of liberty—the ethical time for committing a crime. That's what it's like to be in a rush!

The gaffe gave me a few days' reprieve. So I left without further hindrance…

Around the warden's office, the little streets and docks speak softly, and it's like a transition to the noise of the avenues.

The eighteen months robbed from my life are already in the past.

The present is all that matters.

When a convalescent first goes out, he is flustered. I shook off the lethargy of prison more quickly, because it was so brutal. And now the passersby that I brush against, the traffic noise and the crisp air don't daze me. My step is still familiar with the Parisian pavement.

Where will it lead me?

---

44 The French President assassinated by Italian anarchist Sante Caserio. Caserio's cry before the guillotine was: "Courage, cousins! Long live anarchy!"

To join the anarchists again?

Here I am forced to conclude: I am not an anarchist.

In the criminal court, in the preliminary investigation as well as the hearings, I scorned this explanation. My words of rage and compassion were characterized as anarchist. I did not expound under threat.

Now I want to clarify my first thought, what I have always desired.

It must not fall into vague approximations.

No more grouped into anarchy, than enlisted into socialism. Being a free man, a loner searching beyond; but not enthralled by a dream. Having the pride to affirm myself, outside of schools and sects:

Outside.

The facetious newsmongers commented rather superficially, exclaiming: "But they're inside!" when we were thrown into prison.

And now, above the grayness of all doubts, this appears in the radiance of a vigorous color:

The Will to Live.

And to live outside enslaving laws, outside narrow rules, even outside the theories ideally formulated for the coming age.

To live without believing in a divine paradise or hoping too much for a paradise on earth.

To live for the present, outside of the mirage of future societies; to live and to feel this existence in the arrogant enjoyment of social conflict.

This is more than a state of mind; it is a way of being—here and now.

For too long, men have been led along, by those who show them the conquest of the heavens. We don't even want to wait until we've conquered all the earth.

Let each of us go on for our own enjoyment.

And if there are those who get left along the way, if there are those whom nothing can awaken, if there are innate slaves, people who are incurably debased, so much the worse for them! When you understand this, you go on ahead. And joy lies in acting. We don't have the time to show the way: life is short. As individuals, we rush to the attacks that call us.

Some speak of dilettantism. But this is not without cost, it's not platonic: we pay…

And we start again…